SOUTHERN INFUSED COMFY FOODS

Belinda Slay Ates

Introduction

"Southern Infused Comfy Foods"
If you are a foodie like me, or just enjoy cooking something new in the kitchen, then my hopes are that you will enjoy trying some of my recipes. I challenged my artsy talents and culinary skills to recreate and develop some tasty recipes. However; not to be forgotten, are some worthy and traditional "must share" recipes.

My deepest appreciation to my loving mother, Joan. She raised me with an apron on her waist as she prepared endless and traditonal home cooked meals for our family. She taught me to garden, cook, clean, sew, and love the Lord. I am grateful for her support and encouragment which has helped me through this amazing cookbook journey. Happy cooking and God Bless!
PSALMS 91:2

Belinda Slay Ates

Glossary

Appetizers
Canning & Sauces
Soups & Salads
Entrees & Sides
Desserts

Appetizers

Apple Butter Cream Cheese Dip

Serves 8-12

- [ ] 8 oz. package light cream cheese, softened
- [ ] ½ c. apple butter
- [ ] ½ tsp. vanilla extract
- [ ] ½ tsp. ground cinnamon

Add all ingredients into a mixer. Beat on medium speed for two minutes or well blended and creamy. Refrigerate for 1 hour.

Perfect on toasted bagels.

Apple Fig Crostini

Serves 8-12

- ☐ 6 slices of bacon, cooked and chopped
- ☐ 12 figs, cut in halves
- ☐ 12 baguette or crostini bread slices
- ☐ 4 oz. chevre cheese
- ☐ 4 tbsp. apple butter
- ☐ 1 tbsp. pecans, toasted and chopped
- ☐ 1 tbs. butter, melted
- ☐ 1 tbs. olive oil
- ☐ 1 tsp. salt

Combine olive oil, salt and butter and brush bread with mixture. Toast bread for 2 minutes at 350 degrees. Layer bread with cheese, apple butter, bacon, and pecans. Place fig halves on top of toast. Drizzle with honey on top.

Depending how crispy you like your bread, I prefer 4 minutes at 350 degrees, then allow bread to cool before adding the toppings.

Italian Spinach and Artichoke Spread

Serves 6

- ☐ 1 can drained artichoke hearts, diced
- ☐ 1 lb. Italian sausage, cooked and drained
- ☐ 1 small bag of frozen spinach, thawed and drained
- ☐ 1 packet Knorr's Vegetable Soup Mix
- ☐ 1 packet of dry Ranch dip mix
- ☐ 1 can water chestnuts, drained and diced
- ☐ 1 small yellow onion, minced
- ☐ 2 oz. cream cheese
- ☐ 1 c. mozzarella, shredded
- ☐ 1 c. Parmesan cheese, finely grated
- ☐ 1 c. mayonnaise
- ☐ 1 tsp. of Italian seasonings
- ☐ 1 tsp. fresh lemon juice
- ☐ 1 tsp. Worchester sauce
- ☐ 1 pack of ritz crackers or 1 loaf of garlic toasted baguette

Preheat oven to 350 degrees. Mix all ingredients, except crackers or toast. Place in 8x10 greased baking dish. Bake 45 minutes.

This appetizer brings fond memories of spending time with my dear friend (Katie) in Ohio. She makes amazing stuffed bread similar to this recipe.

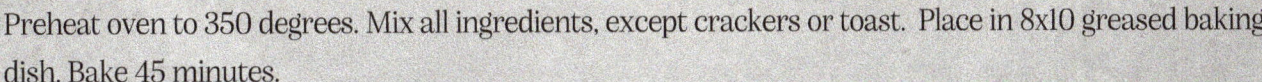

Asparagus and Ham Rollups

Serves 24

- ☐ 2 bunches of fresh asparagus
- ☐ 1 lb. of deli ham, sliced thin
- ☐ 2 tbs. Dijon mustard
- ☐ 2 tbs. herbed cream cheese
- ☐ 2 tsp. of mayonnaise
- ☐ 2 loaves thin white bread

Combine mustard, mayonnaise, and herbed cream cheese and chill for 1 hour.

Clean and trim asparagus ends to approximately 5 inches. Boil asparagus gently in water to cover. Boil 2 minutes for thin asparagus. Dip in ice bath 2 minutes keeping asparagus crispy.

Chill bread for 10 minutes. Cut crust off bread and set aside.

Use a rolling pin flatten out bread. Add mayonnaise mixture, ham, and asparagus. Roll thinly as a cigar look. Place on tray cover and chill for a minimum of 2 hours.

I have also served these at church events using my garlic pickled okra in leu of the asparagus. The ladies seem to love these!

Lobster Filled Avocado

Serves 4

- ☐ ¾ c. diced celery
- ☐ 1 c. lobster meat, cooked
- ☐ ½ c. French dressing
- ☐ 2 avocados
- ☐ 1 green onion, sliced thin
- ☐ ¼ c. Mayonnaise
- ☐ ½ tsp. each salt, pepper, garlic powder, sweet paprika

Marinate lobster in French dressing for ½ hour. Cut avocados in half lengthwise and remove seed. Score the avocado. Drain (not rinsing) French dressing off the lobster. Mix celery, onions, mayonnaise, lobster and seasonings. Fill avocados and cover. Chill a minimum of 30 minutes.

Substitute options: crab meat, shrimp, or salmon

We made these when I served a luncheon to a small group of ladies. I would recommend running lemon juice over the avocado to keep it from browning from oxygen.

Buffalo Chicken Sliders

Serves 12

- [ ] 1 package of Hawaiian sliders, sliced in half
- [ ] 4 c. shredded mozzarella cheese
- [ ] 1 rotisserie chicken discard the skin, debone and shredded
- [ ] 1 bottle Franks Hot Sauce
- [ ] 1 package dry Ranch Dip
- [ ] 8 oz. sour cream
- [ ] 1 tsp. creole seasoning
- [ ] 1 tsp. onion powder
- [ ] 1 package pre-mix coleslaw (carrots, red, and purple cabbage)
- [ ] 1 stick melted butter
- [ ] 1 tsp. celery seeds
- [ ] 1 tsp. garlic, minced
- [ ] 1 tbs. parsley

Combine hot sauce, sour cream, creole seasoning, onion powder, and ranch mix. Combine shredded chicken with cheese and hot sauce mixture. Lightly coat non-stick spray on bottom of pan and tinfoil. Place bottom halves of buns in pan and add chicken mixture. Combine melted butter, celery seeds, garlic, and parsley. Cover tops of slider buns. Bake 350 degrees covered 15 minutes then uncovered 5 more minutes. Before serving, top mix with coleslaw.

*Sliced sweet heat pickles or jalapenos are a hit with these also.

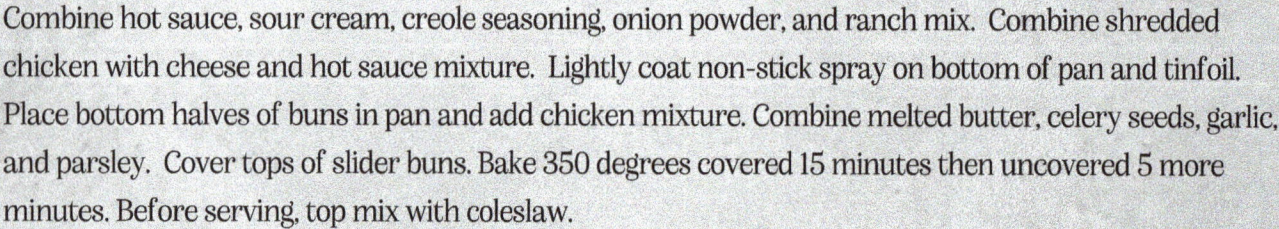

Cajun Bacon Wrapped Dates

Serves 8

- ☐ 16 slices bacon, thin sliced and cut in half
- ☐ 32 dates, pitted
- ☐ 8 oz. Chevre Cheese
- ☐ 1 lemon, juiced
- ☐ 1 tbs. Old Bay or Cajun seasoning
- ☐ 1 tbs. brown sugar
- ☐ 32 toothpicks

Slice dates lengthwise and set aside. Mix cheese, sugar and seasoning. Fill small amounts into each date. Wrap each date and secure with toothpick. Bake in pre-heated 375 degrees oven. Continue rotating the dates from side to side every 10 minutes until the preferred crisp of your bacon. Not recommended to bake longer than 40 minutes. Remove from pan and drizzle the lemon juice. Serve immediately to enjoy warm.

The key is to have thin bacon.

Charcuterie
Tray

Serves 8

- ☐ 8 oz. block cheddar or gouda, cubed

- ☐ 8 oz. block pepperjack, cubed

- ☐ 1 small round brie, sliced like a pizza

- ☐ 8 oz. each pepperoni and salami, sliced

- ☐ 8 oz. sweet deli ham, cubed ½ inch thick

- ☐ 8 oz. smoked deli turkey, cubed ½ inch thick

- ☐ 1 lb. seedless grapes (do not pull from stems)

- ☐ 1 c. blueberries, fresh

- ☐ 1 pint strawberries

- ☐ 8 oz. dried pineapple

- ☐ ½ c. large green olives

- ☐ 2 tbs. fig jam, to cover brie

- ☐ 2 large chocolate bars, broken in square sections

- ☐ 2 sleeves of cracker

- ☐ 2 small sauce cups (for olives and fig jam)

Start with grapes. Begin to place the large items, then smaller size items around your large. Crackers can be mixed in or on the side. Garnish with seasonal decorative fruit or sweet peppers.

At my beautiful niece (Kayton's) wedding, I created a 6 ft. Grazing Charcuterie Table. It takes hours. My sissy, (Debra) and brother (Jim) jumped in to help me and we had a blast creating the table together. #memories #siblings

Crack Chicken Dip

Serves 8

- [ ] 4 boneless chicken breasts or 8 boneless thighs
- [ ] 1 tsp. each garlic (minced), black pepper, and onion powder
- [ ] 2 tsp. parsley
- [ ] 2 c. chicken broth
- [ ] 1 c. water
- [ ] 1 pkg. dry Ranch Seasoning
- [ ] 1 stick of butter, unsalted
- [ ] 2 c. shredded mozzarella
- [ ] 8 oz. cream cheese, softened

Combine all ingredients into a small crockpot. Cook on high for 2 hours, then low for another 2 hours.
Chicken should shred with two forks. Serve with toasted crostini or Ritz crackers.
*Make Crack Chicken sandwiches, add a box of Stove Top Stuffing preparing to directions. Mix stuffing with chicken
to thicken and serve on toasted buns. Don't forget to sprinkle parsley if you like a colorful eye appeal.*

Southern Deviled Eggs

Serves 12

- ☐ 8 eggs
- ☐ 1 tbs. sweet pickle relish
- ☐ 1 tsp. yellow mustard
- ☐ 2 tsp. Thousand Island dressing
- ☐ ¼ cup Mayonnaise
- ☐ ½ tsp. each salt, pepper, celery seed
- ☐ 1 tsp. smoked or regular paprika (for décor)
- ☐ 1 tsp. fresh parsley (for décor)

Bring 8 c. cold water and eggs to boil. Boil for 5 minutes, reduce heat to simmer for additional 15 minutes. Remove from heat and add 8 cubes of ice. Allow eggs to rest for 10 minutes. While eggs are still warm, slightly crush shells peeling under water. Slice eggs lengthwise, separate the yolk from whites. Mash yolks with fork in a medium bowl. Combine ingredients into bowl, reserving paprika and parsley. Gently rinse egg whites and pat dry. Spoon in yolk mixture into egg whites. Top with sprinkled paprika and parsley. Refrigerate 2 hours before serving. Do not allow eggs to sit room temp for more than an hour.

At a young age my Granny Stella sat me down at her dining table and taught me this recipe. She would ask me to make these with her for church and family gatherings over many decades. My niece Hannah is now carrying on the family legacy of Deviled Eggs at our family gatherings. She does an amazing job!

Egg Salad
Finger Sandwiches

Serves 4

- ☐ 8 slices of white bread, thin sliced
- ☐ 4 eggs, hardboiled and peeled
- ☐ ½ c. mayonnaise
- ☐ 1 tsp. yellow mustard
- ☐ 1 tbs. sweet pickle relish, drained
- ☐ 1 tsp. Thousand Island dressing
- ☐ ½ tsp. dry dill or 1 tsp. of fresh chopped dill
- ☐ salt & pepper to taste

Chop eggs finely, add next (6) six ingredients. Place in refrigerator for 30 minutes. Cut edge crust off the bread. Lightly spread mayo on bread then add a small (3) three thin horizontal slices.

To make Tuna Salad Sandwiches, duplicate recipe, reducing to only using (2) two eggs and adding 1 large can of tuna in water, drained.

Garlic Parmesan Crab Stuffed Mushrooms

Serves 16

- [ ] 16 medium mushrooms, portabella
- [ ] 1 lb. fresh crab meat
- [ ] 8 oz. cream cheese, softened
- [ ] 2 tbs. garlic, chopped
- [ ] ½ c. Italian breadcrumbs, lightly toasted for 4 minutes
- [ ] ½ c. shredded parmesan
- [ ] 1 tbs. lemon juice
- [ ] 2 celery stalks, minced
- [ ] 1 tbs. green onion, thinly sliced
- [ ] 1 tsp. each parsley flakes, kosher salt, pepper, paprika
- [ ] Salt and Pepper to taste

Clean mushrooms and remove stems and discard. Preheat oven 350 degrees. Combine all ingredients into a bowl reserving the shredded cheese. Spoon mixture into the mushrooms. Top with shredded cheese. Bake for 20 minutes.

My husband loves it when I add sliced jalapenos and more breadcrumbs on top of shredded cheese, then toasting for additional 5 minutes.

Caprese Skewer
with Balsamic

Serves 12

- ☐ 36 cherry or medley tomatoes
- ☐ 12 skewers (4in. wooden pics)
- ☐ 6 oz. fresh mozzarella balls
- ☐ 24 fresh basil leaves
- ☐ 2 tbs. aged or flavored balsamic
- ☐ 2 tbs. olive oil
- ☐ 1 tsp. kosher salt
- ☐ ½ tsp. crushed black pepper

Wash tomatoes and dry thoroughly. Next, toss them in oil, salt and pepper. Begin the skewer with a tomato, mozzarella, then basil leaf. Repeat again tomato, mozzarella, basil and finish with the third tomato. Once plated on your serving platter, drizzle your favorite aged or flavored balsamic. Chill for 1 hour before serving.

When I make these, I think of my sister Debra, loves these. Try loading them with an olive, a slice of deli salami and cooked (chilled) cheese tortellini.

I use an aged Mission Fig Balsamic. It makes for an Italian burst of flavors.

Holiday Meatballs

Serves 12

- ☐ 2 lbs. of hamburger meat
- ☐ 1 c. brown sugar
- ☐ 1 c. melted butter
- ☐ 1 egg, beaten
- ☐ ¾ c. Italian breadcrumbs
- ☐ ¼ c. milk
- ☐ 1 onion, minced
- ☐ 1 tbs. Worchester Sauce
- ☐ 1 tsp. minced garlic
- ☐ ½ c. *AP flour
- ☐ 1 tsp. salt and pepper, each
- ☐ 1 bottle chili sauce
- ☐ 1 small jar grape jelly

Mix milk, eggs, Worchester sauce, flour, and breadcrumbs to meat. Sautee onions and garlic. Add onion mixture to meat and make into small 1 in. balls. Bake at 350 for 35 minutes. Combine meatballs, chili sauce, and grape jelly in crockpot for 1 hour on high then at low up to 4 hours.

*These were always a staple on Christmas Eve. Mom always put on a big spread for family coming to visit. Christmas is not the same without these special recipes that hold so many warm memories.

Mexican Chicken Dip & Chips

Serves 8-12

- ☐ 4 c. chicken, cooked and cubed
- ☐ 1 large bag of Corn Tortilla Chips
- ☐ 1 c. chicken broth
- ☐ 4 oz. sour cream
- ☐ 4 oz. cream cheese
- ☐ 4 oz. favorite salsa
- ☐ 1 can fire roasted kernel corn
- ☐ 4 c. cheddar cheese, shredded
- ☐ 1 Fajita dry seasoning packet
- ☐ ½ c. melted butter
- ☐ 1 tsp. cumin
- ☐ 1 tsp. paprika
- ☐ 1 tsp. granulated onion
- ☐ 1 tsp. cilantro & lime seasoning
- ☐ 1 can Rotel, drained

Coat crock pot with non-stock spray. Add all ingredients. Slow cook for 1 hour on medium or low heat.

My lovely niece Haley loved to have this dip when she would come over to visit. I knew to have this ready when she would come for a sleep over. #aunt-neice #fun

Mississippi Chicken Sliders

Serves 6

- [ ] 8 chicken thighs or 4 chicken breasts, cleaned and fat pulled
- [ ] 8 oz. cream cheese
- [ ] 1 pkg. Ranch, dry
- [ ] 1 pkg. Au Jus, dry
- [ ] 1 tsp. garlic, minced
- [ ] 1 stick of non-salted butter
- [ ] 2 c. chicken broth
- [ ] 1 small jar pecorino peppers
- [ ] salt & pepper to taste
- [ ] 12 slider buns

Combine all ingredients into a medium size crockpot, including the juice from the peppers. Cook on low for 4 hours or high for 2 hours. The internal temperature should reach 165 degrees. Chicken will shred with fork. Stir blending everything after shredding. Let sit for 10 minutes while you toast up your favorite sliders. Enjoy!

These are perfect for game days! Our son loves these on Hawaiian slider buns, so I always make extra.

Rueben Sandwiches

Serves 8

- ☐ 1 stick of butter
- ☐ 1 jar or package sauerkraut, drained
- ☐ 4 tbs. Thousand Island dressing
- ☐ 8 slices of bread of choice
- ☐ 1 lb. sliced corned beef, sliced thin
- ☐ 8 slices Swiss cheese
- ☐ 1 tbs. coarse deli mustard
- ☐ ½ package onion soup mix
- ☐ 2 tsp. poppy seeds

Preheat oven to 350 degrees. Spray 9x11 pan. Combine dressing, mustard, and sauerkraut. Melt butter with onion soup mix and poppy seeds then brush over bread slices. Begin to layer on pan, cheese, sauerkraut mixture, corned beef, and add remaining 4 more slices of cheese before top bread slice.
Cover with foil, bake for 25 minutes. Uncover the last 5 minutes for a toasty finish.

These are a hit for St Patty's Day appetizer when cut into halves or quartered. Try fresh baked rye marble bread.

Shrimp Salad on Brioche Buns

Serves 4

- ☐ 4 brioche hotdog buns
- ☐ ½ c. mayo (extra for the bun)
- ☐ 2 oz. herbal or chives cream cheese
- ☐ 1 tbs. cocktail sauce
- ☐ 1 large celery stalk, diced
- ☐ 2 tbs. chopped dill (extra for garnish)
- ☐ 1 tbs. fresh squeezed lemon
- ☐ 1 tbs. sweet relish
- ☐ 1 tbs. fresh chives, chopped
- ☐ 1 tsp. sea salt and pepper
- ☐ ¼ tsp. Old Bay Seasoning
- ☐ 1 lb. fresh cooked medium shrimp
- ☐ 4 large Bibb lettuce leaves
- ☐ Hot sauce for taste

Blend mayo, cocktail and cream cheese until smooth. Combine the mayo mixture, celery, dill, lemon, relish, chives, seasonings to the shrimp. Spread mayo, add lettuce then top with shrimp mixture. Enjoy with your favorite crispy chip.

These are great for a summer picnic by the lake. I also make a strawberry-pineapple lemonade to pair nicely with this recipe.

Smoked Gouda Pimento Cheese Sandwiches

Serves 4

- ☐ 8 slices of white or wheat bread, thin sliced
- ☐ 1 c. mayonnaise
- ☐ 2 oz. cream cheese, softened
- ☐ 1 c. cheddar cheese, shredded
- ☐ 1 c. smoked gouda cheese, shredded
- ☐ 1 tbs. pimentos, drained and diced
- ☐ 1 tsp. yellow mustard
- ☐ 1 tsp. Thousand Island dressing
- ☐ 1 tsp. Worcestershire sauce
- ☐ 1 tsp. hot sauce
- ☐ 1 tsp. paprika
- ☐ 1 tsp. sugar
- ☐ Salt & pepper to taste

Blend cream cheese, mayo, mustard, and Thousand Island dressing. Add remaining ingredients. Refrigerate for 30 minutes. Lightly spread mayo on bread then add pimento cheese spread.

Classic Favorite of mine when served on toasted Jalapeno Cheddar Bread.

Jalapeno Pimento Cheese Poppers

Serves 8

- ☐ 4 jalapenos, cut in half and seeded
- ☐ 8 thin slices of bacon
- ☐ ½ c. mayonnaise
- ☐ 2 oz. cream cheese, softened
- ☐ 1 c. cheddar cheese, shredded
- ☐ 1 c. smoked gouda cheese, shredded
- ☐ 1 tbs. pimentos, drained and diced
- ☐ 1 tsp. yellow mustard
- ☐ 1 tsp. hot sauce
- ☐ 1 tsp. paprika
- ☐ 1 tsp. sugar
- ☐ Salt & pepper to taste

Blend all ingredients reserving the jalapenos and bacon. Chill the pimento cheese mixture for 30 minutes. Cut the jalapenos length wise, remove seeds and stems. Blanch jalapenos in boiling water for 2 minutes. Stuff jalapenos with the cream cheese mixture, then wrap with bacon. Place on a sprayed cookie sheet and back 400 degrees for 20 minutes.

I offer a sweet chili dipping sauce along with ranch. FABULOUS football game day treats!

Dry Rub Smoked Chicken Wings

Serves 8

- ☐ 4 lbs. chicken wings
- ☐ 3 c. water
- ☐ ½ c. Worcestershire sauce
- ☐ ¼ c. brown sugar
- ☐ ¼ c. kosher salt
- ☐ 2 c. seasonings of choice
- ☐ 2 tbs. *BP (baking powder)

Wash and clean wings. Brine wings with all liquids, sugar, and salt for 1 hour. Rinse and pat dry. Lightly dust the wings in the baking powder. Add dry rub seasonings of choice on all sides of wings. Smoke on high temp of 350 for 30 minutes. Reduce smoke temp to 180 degrees for two (2) hours.

*Do not use frozen wings. Sprinkling baking powder is a great way to crisp up the wings before you cook them.

*I created a dry rub seasoning with equal amounts of Greek seasoning, granulated garlic and onion powder.

Stuffed Banana Peppers

Serves 6-8

- ☐ 12 large banana peppers
- ☐ 8 oz. cream cheese
- ☐ 1 c. shredded mozzarella
- ☐ ½ lb. Italian sausage, browned, drained, and cooled
- ☐ ½ small green onion, sliced thinly
- ☐ 1 tsp. each salt, black pepper, garlic powder

Combine cream cheese and mozzarella with dry seasonings and sausage. Trim the tops off the peppers then core removing seeds and ribs. Pipe the cream cheese mixture into the peppers. Chill for 2 hours minimum. Slice into bite size pieces.

These pair well when sliced thin, placed on crackers and topped with pepper jelly. Be daring and add minced pickled jalapenos.

Super Bowl Dip & Chips

Serves 8-12

- ☐ 1 lbs. pork sausage, browned and drained
- ☐ 1 lb. hamburger meat, browned and drained
- ☐ 1 large bag of corn tortilla chips
- ☐ 8 oz. sour cream
- ☐ 8 oz. mayonnaise
- ☐ 4 oz. cream cheese
- ☐ 8 oz. favorite salsa
- ☐ 1 large tomato, diced
- ☐ 1 can Rotel, drained
- ☐ 3 c. cheddar cheese, fresh shredded
- ☐ 2 c. Mexican blend shredded cheese
- ☐ 1 fajita or taco dry seasoning packet
- ☐ 1 tsp. each cumin, paprika, onion powder
- ☐ 2 tsp. fresh cilantro

Blend sour cream and cream cheese. Add salsa and remaining ingredients. Chill for 2 hours then serve.

Our son-in-law Calvin always requests this dip for the past decade of Super Bowls and his birthdays.

Tzatziki Dip

Serves 4

- ☐ 1 English cucumber, diced
- ☐ 4 scallions, sliced minced
- ☐ 1 garlic glove, minced
- ☐ 1 c. plain Greek yogurt
- ☐ 3 tbs. mint, chopped
- ☐ Salt & pepper to taste

Combine all ingredients reserving 1 tbs. of mint to sprinkle on top. Cover and chill for 1 hour before serving.

Pita chips and fresh veggies are a perfect pairing.

Ranch Chicken Sliders

Serves 6

- ☐ 8 chicken thighs, boneless, skinless
- ☐ 1 package of Hawaiian sliders
- ☐ ½ stick butter, melted
- ☐ 1 can cream of mushrooms
- ☐ 2 c. crushed Ritz crackers
- ☐ 1 medium onion, chopped
- ☐ 1 cup sour cream
- ☐ 1 c. shredded cheddar cheese
- ☐ 4 oz. cream cheese
- ☐ 1 Ranch dry package
- ☐ salt & pepper to taste

Combine all ingredients into crockpot reserving the sliders to serve. Cook on low setting 4 hours. Chicken will shred easily. Allow to sit for 10 minutes then serve with slider buns.

Smoked Mini Cheese Balls

Serves 8

☐ 16 oz of cream cheese

☐ 1 c. seasonings of choice

Allow cream cheese to come to room temperature for at least an hour. Roll small balls in the palm of your hand (no bigger than the nickel size). Place balls on parchment paper then roll the balls in your favorite seasonings. Return cheese balls to the parchment paper on a pan. Place in smoker for 150-180 degrees for 2 hours. Serve with buttery crackers.

House favorite Cajun or Brown Sugar and BBQ Rub seasoning. Other favorites include Old Bay seasoning, Everything Bagel, Italian herbs, and cinnamon with sugar.

If you do not have a smoker, it will be okay as you can still make these. The smoke flavor is just a bonus.

Mediterranean Grilled Chicken on Crackers

Serves 12

- ☐ 1 package of your favorite crispy crackers
- ☐ 4 c. diced grilled chicken
- ☐ 1 container of hummus
- ☐ 4 oz. tzatziki
- ☐ 4 small tomatoes, sliced small
- ☐ 1 tsp. onion powder
- ☐ 1/4 c. fresh red onions, thinly sliced or pickled red onions
- ☐ 1 tbs. parsley
- ☐ 1 tbs. Greek seasoning
- ☐ 2 tbs. crumbled feta
- ☐ 1 lemon, thinly sliced
- ☐ 1 tbs. fresh dill for garnish

Combine Tzatziki and Greek seasoning. Layer the hummus as the base on the cracker. Top with veggies and grilled chicken. Lastly add a dallop of tzatziki and sprinkle with feta cheese crumbles and garnish with fresh dill.

Canning & Sauces

Granny's Apple Butter

Makes 8 Pints

- ☐ 15 lbs. fresh gala apples, peeled and cored
- ☐ 5 ½ c. brown sugar
- ☐ 4 c. granulated sugar
- ☐ 2 tbs. ground cinnamon
- ☐ 1 tsp. each salt and cinnamon extract
- ☐ ½ tsp. ground cloves
- ☐ ½ tsp. nutmeg
- ☐ 1 c. red hot candies
- ☐ 1 c. boiling water

Bring apples and vinegar to boil. Reduce and simmer uncovered 30 minutes until tender. Remove from heat and use immersion blender until smooth. Add sugars, ground cinnamon, and spices. Boil red hot in water until dissolved then stir into apples. Bring that mixture to boil, then simmer uncovered for 2 hours. Ladle into pint jars, wipe lids clean (leaving ½ inch headspace). Cover with hot water bath and simmer on boil for 5 minutes.

Store unsealed jars in refrigerator for up to 2 months.

Blueberry Jam

Makes 10 Half Pints

- ☐ 16 c. fresh blueberries, washed
- ☐ 6 c. sugar
- ☐ ½ c. water
- ☐ 1 tsp. lemon, fresh squeezed

Bring all ingredients to boil over medium heat in a non-stick pot. Stir frequently often. Reduce heat to medium-low for 1 hour. Stirring frequently, removing the foam from the top of pot. Do NOT let jam become sticky which requires more stirring after 30 minutes. Quickly process in jars, packing tightly under the neck of jar. Wipe lids and seal in hot-water bath for 10 minutes.

Refrigerate unsealed jars for up to 2 months.

Candied Jalapenos aka Cowboy Candy

Makes 4-5 Half Pints

- [ ] 1 lb. fresh jalapenos, seeded and sliced thin
- [ ] ¾ c. apple cider vinegar
- [ ] 2 ½ c. granulated sugar
- [ ] 1 tsp. granulated garlic powder
- [ ] 1 tsp. celery seed
- [ ] 1 tsp. turmeric
- [ ] ½ tsp. red pepper flakes

Combine all ingredients reserving jalapenos in a non-stick pot. Boil for 5 minutes. Stir in jalapenos and cook for another 5 minutes stirring constantly. Remove from heat and pack peppers into clean jars, not past the neck. Wipe lids clean and seal. Place in refrigerator 24 hours before serving.

Store in refrigerator for up to 2 months.

Fancy Honey-Nut Butter

Makes 1 c.

- ☐ ½ c. butter
- ☐ ½ c. honey
- ☐ ½. c. pecans, minced

Cream butter with a blender until light and fluffy. Slowly add honey as blending. Stir in nuts.

Will keep refrigerated for up to 7 days. Excellent on bagels and muffins.

Fig Jam

Makes 2 pints

- ☐ 2 lbs. fresh figs, washed and quartered
- ☐ 2 c. sugar
- ☐ ½ c. water
- ☐ 1 lemon, juiced
- ☐ 1 tsp. vanilla

Discard any stems from the figs. Combine ingredients into a medium non-aluminum saucepan. Cover and cook over medium heat, stirring frequently until figs become tender and soft. Uncover and simmer for 20 minutes. Remove from heat and let stand 1 hour. Pour into 2-pint jars. Store in refrigerator for up to 2 months. Recipe may make more depending on the size of the figs.

My Aunt Mary Lou enjoys this recipe when I make these for the holidays. She is so thoughtful; she gave me a mission fig tree! #love

Green Tomato Chutney

Makes 2 Pints

- ☐ 1 lb. green tomatoes, peeled, chopped
- ☐ 1 lb. green apples, peeled, diced
- ☐ 2 medium white onions, sliced thin
- ☐ 2 ½ c. white wine vinegar
- ☐ 2 c. golden raisins
- ☐ 2 ½ c. brown sugar
- ☐ 2 c. water
- ☐ 4 garlic cloves, minced
- ☐ 1 tsp. each ginger, coarse black pepper, cinnamon, nutmeg
- ☐ 1 tbs. kosher salt

Combine all ingredients in a coated pot. Bring to a boil for 5 minutes, simmer heat to low stirring often until most liquid has evaporated but still covering chutney. Pour chutney ½ inch below jar neck and pack tightly. Wipe rim clean and apply lid. Process in hot-water bath (covers the lids) for 15 minutes. Set on counter to seal overnight.

If jars do not seal, place in refrigerator for up to 1 month.

Hot Pepper Jelly

Makes 5-6 Half Pints

- ☐ 5 c. fresh jalapenos, seeded and minced
- ☐ 1 ¼ c. apple cider vinegar
- ☐ ¾ c. red peppers, seeded and minced
- ☐ 6 c. granulated sugar
- ☐ ¼ c. lime juice. apple juice
- ☐ 1.75 oz powdered pectin = 3 oz. liquid
- ☐ 1 tsp. salt

Combine all ingredients EXCEPT pectin into non-stick pot. Boil for 10 minutes. Stir in pectin and boil for 1 minute stirring constantly. Remove from heat and cool. Pack peppers jelly into hot sterile jars, NOT past the neck. Wipe lids clean and seal. Cover with water just over lids. Bring to a light boil and simmer for 10 minutes.

Store unsealed jelly in refrigerator for up to 2 months.

Strawberry/Rhubarb Jam

Makes 4 cups

- [ ] 3 c. rhubarb, diced
- [ ] 1 pkg. 3oz of wild strawberry Jello, dry
- [ ] 3 c. sugar
- [ ] 1 tsp. vanilla

Combine all ingredients in saucepan except strawberry Jello. Bring to boil, then reduce heat to simmer. Simmer for 20 minutes. Remove from heat and stir in Jello. Let stand 5 minutes. Pour into jars and let stand to cool. Keep refrigerated up to 2 months.

Pickled Sweet
Red Onions

Makes 4 pints

- ☐ 2 red onions, large and sliced thin

- ☐ 4 c. sugar white granulated sugar

- ☐ 1 c. water

- ☐ 2 c. apple cider vinegar

- ☐ 1 jalapeno, sliced thin

- ☐ 1 tsp. garlic salt

- ☐ 1 tbs. sea salt

- ☐ 1 tbs. crushed red pepper flakes

Fill 4 pints with red onions, jalapenos, and red pepper flakes. Make sure each jar is packed tightly. Combine remaining ingredients in boiling pot. Bring to boil, stirring constantly. Reduce and simmer for 10 minutes, stirring frequently. Fill each jar to cover the onions. Allow jars to cool for 1 hour, then apply lids and refrigerate for up to 2 months. These will be ready to snack on within 48 hours.

Soaking your onions in an ice bath helps reduce the gas from the onions and lessens the bitterness taste. Rosemary can be added for an enhanced flavor.

Sweet Heat Refrigerated Pickles

Makes 4 pints

- ☐ 4 medium cucumbers, washed, sliced thin
- ☐ 4 c. sugar
- ☐ 1 c. water
- ☐ 2 c. apple cider vinegar
- ☐ 1 red onion, sliced thin and soaked in ice water bath (at least 5 minutes)
- ☐ 1 jalapeno, sliced thin
- ☐ 1 tsp. garlic salt
- ☐ 1 tbs. sea salt
- ☐ 1 tbs. crushed red pepper flakes
- ☐ 1 tsp. celery seed
- ☐ 2 tbs. fresh dill weed

Fill 4-pint jars with cucumbers, red onions, garlic, jalapenos, and red pepper flakes. Make sure each jar is packed tightly. Combine the remaining ingredients into a boiling pot. Bring to boil, stirring constantly. Reduce and simmer for 10 minutes, stirring frequently. Fill each jar with hot liquid mixture. Allow jars to cool for 1 hour, then apply lids and refrigerate for up to 2 months. These will be ready to snack on within 48 hours.

If you do not have fresh dill, use half the amount of dried dill. Ed Hall, (friend and former boss) loves these and my regular Garlic Dills. I would brig some to work and it seemed to brighten his day a bit.

Pesto
Mayo

Makes 1 Pints

- ☐ 1 pt. mayo
- ☐ 2 tbs. pesto
- ☐ 1 tsp. sundried tomato sauce
- ☐ ½ tsp. kosher salt
- ☐ 1 tsp. onion powder
- ☐ 1 tsp. garlic powder

Mix all ingredients together and cover. Allow to chill a minimum of 1 hour before serving.

My nephew Cody explores many dishes with this pesto mayo. One fabulous dish he made was using this mayo on a steak sandwich.

Coleslaw Dressing

Makes 2 cups

- ☐ 1 lemon juice, fresh squeezed
- ☐ 2 c. mayonnaise
- ☐ ½ c. granulated sugar
- ☐ ½ c. apple cider vinegar
- ☐ 1 tbs. poppy seeds

Mix all ingredients together and cover.

Combine vinegar, lemon juice, and sugar together then add mayo and poppyseeds. Allow to chill a minimum 30 minutes.

Don't skip on the brand quality of mayo, it makes a difference.

Breakfast
Sausage Gravy

Serves 4

- ☐ 16 oz. pork breakfast sausage, browned, drained, crumbled
- ☐ 1 ½ tbs. sausage grease renderings
- ☐ 2 ½ c. milk
- ☐ ½ c. AP* flour
- ☐ ½ tsp. sugar
- ☐ ¼ tsp. pepper
- ☐ ¼ tsp. ground sage
- ☐ ½ tsp. salt
- ☐ ½ tsp. All Purpose Greek seasoning

Slowly whisk flour in rendered hot sausage grease on med high. Continue to whisk until smooth for
1 minute. Once thick, gradually add in milk, whisking constantly for 5-7 minutes or until thickened again.
Stir in sausage, sugar, and seasonings. Add small amounts of milk if it is too thick.

We like to sprinkle Sweet Smoked Paprika to décor. This gravy is perfect with ladling over biscuits or grits.

Spaghetti Sauce

Makes 6

- [ ] 1 small can of tomato paste
- [ ] 1 tsp. each Italian seasoning, Oregano, Basil, Parsley
- [ ] ¼ tsp. salt
- [ ] 1 c. water
- [ ] 2 beef bouillon cubes
- [ ] 2 bay leaves
- [ ] 2 cans tomato sauce
- [ ] 1 can tomato puree
- [ ] 1 tbs. crushed garlic
- [ ] ½ small red onion, minced
- [ ] 1 lb. Italian sausage, cooked and drained
- [ ] 1 lb. hamburger, browned and drained
- [ ] ½ tsp. pepper
- [ ] 2 tbs. fresh parsley, chopped

Combine all ingredients into a crockpot. Allow to slow cook for 3 hours. Serve over your favorite pasta, then lightly sprinkle with fresh parsley.

Sometimes, I make this recipe with ground turkey and ground pork. I will omit the beef and Italian sausage. It seems lighter and healthier.

Sweet & Savory BBQ Sauce

Serves 12

- ☐ ½ stick butter
- ☐ 6 oz. soy sauce
- ☐ 2 c. brown sugar
- ☐ 1 jalapeno pepper, minced
- ☐ 2 c. ketchup
- ☐ 2 tbs. yellow mustard
- ☐ 1 tbs. Crystals Hot Sauce
- ☐ 1 tsp. Worcestershire sauce
- ☐ 1 tsp. each onion powder and garlic powder
- ☐ salt & pepper to taste

Melt butter in saucepan. Combine ingredients and bring to a boil. Simmer for 10 minutes. Allow it to cool before placing sauce in refrigerator.

Chipotle Diablo Hot Sauce

Makes 4 cups

- ☐ 2 small cans of Chipotle Peppers in Adobo sauce
- ☐ 2 c. Chicken Broth
- ☐ 4 tbsp. butter
- ☐ 1 tsp. onion powder
- ☐ 1 tsp. garlic powder

Combine all ingredients in saucepan. Bring to boil, then reduce heat to simmer.   Simmer for 20 minutes. Use an emersion blender or countertop blender to puree.

Best served on top of BBQ Pork or Chicken. We also add 1 tbsp. of sauce to 1 cup of mayo to add on sandwiches. Yummy!

Southern Pepper Sauce

Makes 1 Pints

- ☐ 1 pint hot peppers, washed and dried
- ☐ 1 c. vinegar

Heat vinegar to boil. Fill pint jar with hot peppers. Cover peppers with hot vinegar. Seal with lid immediately. Room temperature or refrigeration is optional.

New Orleans Remoulade Sauce

Makes 1 ½ cups

- ☐ 1 c. mayo
- ☐ 2 tbs. Dijon mustard
- ☐ 1 tbs. lemon juice (fresh squeezed)
- ☐ 1 tbs. fresh parsley, chopped
- ☐ 1 tbs. hot sauce (your favorite)
- ☐ 2 tsp. whole-grain mustard
- ☐ 2 garlic cloves, minced
- ☐ 1 tsp. Worcestershire sauce
- ☐ 1 tsp. paprika
- ☐ ½ tsp. kosher salt
- ☐ ¼ tsp. cayenne pepper

Mix all ingredients together and cover. Allow to chill 1 hour before serving.

Tartar Sauce

Makes 2 cups

- [ ] ½ white onion, diced
- [ ] 1 large green onion, minced
- [ ] ½ c. sweet pickle relish
- [ ] 1 tbs. of lemon juice
- [ ] 2 tsp. yellow mustard
- [ ] 2 tsp. dill weed
- [ ] 2 c. Mayonnaise

Mix all ingredients together and cover. Allow to chill a minimum of 1 hour.

When making this tartar sauce try making the night before. I found it really enriches the zest of the lemon.

Keep refrigerated and discard after 5 days.

Medium White Sauce

Makes 1 cup

☐ 2 tbs. butter

☐ 2 tbs. all-purpose flour

☐ 1 cup milk

☐ ½ tsp salt

☐ ½ tsp pepper

Melt butter, remove from heat. Add flour and mix until smooth. Add milk and seasoning allow cooking on simmer until thickened stirring constantly cover.

*Cheese Sauce- add ½ cup shredded cheese
*Cream Sauce- use cream instead of milk
*Lobster Sauce- add 1 cup of diced cooked lobster meat
*Bercy Sauce- cook 1 tbls of diced shallots in butter before adding the flour, use fish stock instead of the milk
*Oyster Sauce- cook 1 cup of oysters in their liquid until plump, drain liquid and use for part of the milk in White Sauce, add oysters just before serving
*Drawn Butter Sauce- use hot water or fish stock instead of milk in White Sauce, add 2 tbls of butter to thicken
*White Sauce with Egg- add 1 sliced hard-boiled egg to Butter Sauce

Soups & Salads

Broccoli Cheddar Soup

8 Servings

- [ ] 2 tbs. vegetable oil or butter
- [ ] 2 tbs. *AP flour
- [ ] 4 chicken bouillon cubes
- [ ] 6 c. water
- [ ] 1 large head of broccoli, diced and steamed
- [ ] 1 c. Monterey Jack cheese, shredded
- [ ] 1 c. cheddar cheese, shredded
- [ ] 1 can of evaporated milk (or 1.5 cups of room temp 2% milk)
- [ ] salt & pepper to taste

Bring bouillon cubes and water to a boil. In a separate non-stick boiling pot sprinkle flour stirring consistently for a few minutes until golden. Add oil/butter to the flour and whisk together slowly. Once it becomes thick and smooth add 1 cup of broth at a time whisking vigorously. Add remaining ingredients except the milk. Bring to boil, not burning the bottom at this stage. Once boiling, turn temp to low. Simmer for 20 minutes. Use an immersion blender to puree the broccoli and add milk to soup.

Adding the milk at the very end will ensure no curdling. Mom taught me how to make this many decades ago. Our son loves this soup in the Fall.

Pumpkin
Turkey Chili

Serves 8

- ☐ 1 ½ teaspoons olive oil
- ☐ 1 lb. ground turkey
- ☐ 1 onion, chopped
- ☐ 2 c. water
- ☐ 28 oz. can tomatoes. crushed
- ☐ 16 oz. can cannellini beans, drained
- ☐ 1 tbs. garlic, minced
- ☐ 3 tbs. dark chili powder
- ☐ ½ tsp. paprika, dried oregano, black pepper, cumin
- ☐ 1 chipotle pepper in adobo
- ☐ 1 tbs. ground cumin
- ☐ 2 tsp. salt
- ☐ 2 c. pumpkin or butternut squash, peeled and diced

Heat the oil in a large pot over medium heat. Place turkey in the pot and cook until evenly brown. Stir in onion and cook until tender. Pour the water into the pot. Mix in tomatoes, white beans, pumpkin, and garlic. Season chili powder, paprika, oregano, chipotle, cumin, salt, and pepper. Bring to a boil. Reduce heat to low, cover, and simmer 30 minutes.

My mother shared this recipe with me. I am so glad she did, this recipe is excellent in the winter!

Classic Chicken Noodle Soup

Serves 4

- [ ] 1 lb. egg noodles
- [ ] 1 small onion, diced
- [ ] 1 tbs. garlic, minced
- [ ] 1 c. celery, diced
- [ ] 2 large potatoes, diced
- [ ] 2 small carrots, sliced thin
- [ ] 1 lb. raw chicken thighs or breast
- [ ] 4 c. hot water
- [ ] 2 c. chicken stock
- [ ] 2 c. vegetable stock
- [ ] 1 tbs. butter
- [ ] ½ tsp. onion powder
- [ ] 1 tsp. poultry seasoning
- [ ] 2 large Bay Leaves
- [ ] 1 tbs. fresh parsley and thyme
- [ ] salt & pepper to taste

In a large stove top pot, sauté the onions, carrots, celery, and seasonings in butter for 5 minutes. Add remaining ingredients reserving egg noodles. Cook on med high for 10 minutes. Remove chicken and chop into bite size pieces. Add chicken and egg noodles to the soup. Continue cooking for an additional 20 minutes. Pull out Bay leaves before serving.

Cream of Potato Cheddar & Smoked Gouda Soup

Serves 8

- ☐ 4 c. potatoes, diced bite size
- ☐ 2 c. water
- ☐ 2 c. chicken broth
- ☐ 2 c. shredded cheddar
- ☐ 2 c. shredded smoked gouda
- ☐ 1 c. onions, diced
- ☐ ¾ c. celery, diced
- ☐ 2 tbs. butter
- ☐ 2 oz. softened cream cheese
- ☐ 8 oz. half and half milk
- ☐ 2 tbs. cornstarch
- ☐ 1 tsp. onion powder
- ☐ 1 tsp. each sea salt or kosher salt, black pepper, parsley

Combine potatoes, onions, celery, seasonings, chicken broth and water to a large stock pot. Bring to boil then reduce temperature to slow cook for 5 minutes. Remove and set aside 1 c. of potatoes pieces. In a separate bowl, whisk 2 tbs. corn starch with 2 tbs. cold water, stir until smooth. Add cornstarch mix, cheeses, cream cheese, sour cream and milk into soup mixture. Use an immersion blender to blend smooth with a thick consistency, not thin. Add the remaining potatoes to the soup. Continue on a low boil for 10 minutes.

Great with fresh chives and chopped crispy bacon pieces garnished on top.

Hamburger Soup

Serves 4

- ☐ 1 lb. hamburger meat, browned, drained
- ☐ 1 small onion, diced
- ☐ 1 tsp. garlic, minced
- ☐ 1 c. celery, diced
- ☐ 1 c. carrots, sliced thin
- ☐ 4 c. hot water
- ☐ 4 c. beef stock
- ☐ 1 lb. macaroni
- ☐ 1 can of tomato soup
- ☐ 1 tbs. butter
- ☐ 1 tbs. granulated sugar
- ☐ ½ tsp. onion powder
- ☐ salt & pepper to taste

In a large stove top pot, sauté the onions, carrots, celery, and seasonings in butter for 5 minutes. Next add remaining ingredients reserving the noodles. Bring to a boil then simmer for 10 minutes. Add noodles and cook for another 20 minutes.

*If you prefer, add 1 cup of whole kernel sweet corn along with other veggies.

Holiday Oyster Stew

Serves 6

- ☐ 1 15 oz. can evaporated milk
- ☐ 2 c. water
- ☐ 1 pint fresh oysters
- ☐ ½ stick of butter
- ☐ salt & pepper to taste
- ☐ pinch of fresh chives and dill

Rinse and drain oysters in colander. Add all ingredients and bring to slow boil for 10 minutes. Reduce heat and simmer for an additional 10 minutes. Add a pinch of fresh chives and dill on top on soup before serving.

My Granny Tillman taught my mom this recipe when she was very young. From what I can find out, this recipe dates to the 1800's in my family. Such a fabulous treat when my mom makes this during the winter holidays. I add a touch of Old Bay seasoning to my bowl.

Old Fashion Vegetable Soup

Serves 8

- ☐ 1 ham bone
- ☐ 1 small onion, diced
- ☐ 1 c. celery, diced
- ☐ 1 c. potatoes, peeled and diced
- ☐ 1 c. field peas or early peas
- ☐ 1 can sweet cream corn
- ☐ 1 c. baby carrots
- ☐ 2 c. hot water
- ☐ 8 c. vegetable stock
- ☐ 15 oz. can crushed tomatoes
- ☐ 2 tbs. butter
- ☐ 1 pkg. Knorr's vegetable soup mix
- ☐ salt, pepper and thyme to taste

Combine all ingredients into a slow cooker. Cook on high for one (1) hour and then on low for another three (3) hours.

Great with homemade cornbread or crackers. Can use ham bone left over from holidays.

Hearty Sausage Kale Soup

Serves 4

- ☐ 1 lb. Italian Sausage, browned and drained
- ☐ 1 small onion, diced
- ☐ 1 tbs. garlic, minced
- ☐ 1 c. celery, diced
- ☐ 4 large potatoes, diced
- ☐ 2 small carrots, sliced thin
- ☐ 2 c. kale, chopped
- ☐ 4 c. hot water
- ☐ 2 c. beef stock
- ☐ 2 c. vegetable stock
- ☐ 1 can of diced tomatoes
- ☐ 1 tbs. butter
- ☐ ½ tsp. onion powder
- ☐ salt & pepper to taste
- ☐ 1 can evaporated milk.

In a large stove top pot, sauté the onions, carrots, celery, and seasonings in butter for 8 minutes. Add water, broth, garlic, diced tomatoes, sausage, and kale. Slow cook on med high for 25 minutes. Last 5 minutes add milk.

Seafood Chowder

Serves 4-6

- ☐ 2 lbs. fresh or frozen white fish fillets, cut bite size
- ☐ 1 lb. fresh shrimp, peeled
- ☐ 1 lb. fresh bay scallops
- ☐ 2 tbs. fresh lemon juice
- ☐ ½ lb. bacon, diced
- ☐ 1 onion, medium size, diced
- ☐ 4 potatoes, medium size, cubed
- ☐ 2 Bay leaves
- ☐ 1 celery stalk, thinly sliced
- ☐ 1 tsp. parsley flakes
- ☐ 2 c. water
- ☐ 2 c. chicken broth
- ☐ 1 can clams
- ☐ 1.5 tsp. salt
- ☐ 1 tbs. Old Bay seasoning
- ☐ ¼ tsp. pepper
- ☐ 1 can evaporated milk

Sautee bacon, celery, and onions in butter. Next combine all ingredients reserving shrimp and scallops into a crock pot including the bacon fat. Cook on high for 1 hour, reduce the temp to low for another hour. Last 30 minutes stir in shrimp and scallops.

Tomato Basil Soup

12 Servings

- [ ] 2 tbs. vegetable oil or butter
- [ ] 4 c. vegetable broth
- [ ] 4 c. water
- [ ] 8 large tomatoes, quartered
- [ ] 2 tbs. pesto
- [ ] 2 tbs. cornstarch
- [ ] 2 tbs. cold water
- [ ] 1 tbs. sundried tomato paste
- [ ] 1 can of evaporated milk

   (or 1.5 cups of room temp 2% milk)

- [ ] salt & pepper to taste

All ingredients in a large non-stick boiling pot, reserving the milk until last 5 minutes of cooking. Bring to boil, reduce heat to medium-high for 20 minutes. Use an immersion blender to puree. Next whisk cornstarch and cold water in a small bowl until smooth. Add cornstarch and milk to soup.

Serve with garlic croutons on top of soup in bowls.

White Chicken Chili Soup

12 Servings

- [ ] 6 chicken bouillon cubes
- [ ] 8 c. water
- [ ] 2 cans pinto chili beans, drained
- [ ] 1 can kidney chili beans, drained
- [ ] 1 can black beans, drained
- [ ] 1 can sweet corn, drained
- [ ] 4 chicken breasts, chopped
- [ ] 8 oz. cream cheese
- [ ] 1 package of white chicken chili mix
- [ ] ½ c. white sugar
- [ ] 2 tbs. cumin
- [ ] 2 tsp. granulated garlic
- [ ] 2 tbs. cilantro
- [ ] 1 tbs. paprika
- [ ] salt & pepper to taste
- [ ] Add at end 1 can of evaporated milk

Place chicken in crockpot, adding all ingredients except milk on top of chicken. Slow cook on high for 3 hours or low 5 hours. Before serving, stir milk last 5 minutes into soup.

A great recipe our daughter can throw together in a snap! She has the touch for a great tasting chili.

Cream of Zucchini Soup

Serves 4

- ☐ 3 medium sliced zucchinis
- ☐ 4 c. water
- ☐ 2 c. vegetable broth
- ☐ ½ small onion, minced
- ☐ 1 tsp. each minced garlic, dried tarragon, dried parsley flakes
- ☐ 4 chicken bouillon cubes
- ☐ 2 tbs. butter
- ☐ 2 tbs. flour
- ☐ ½ tsp. onion powder
- ☐ salt & pepper to taste
- ☐ 2 c. half and half
- ☐ 2 tbs. sour cream
- ☐ 1 tsp. smoked or sweet paprika

In a large saucepan combine zucchinis, water, onion, parsley, and chicken bullions. Cook on med high 5 minutes. Pour into blender or use an immersion blender to puree. Melt butter in saucepan and add flour, tarragon, salt, and pepper. Create a roux on medium-low by stirring consistently, cook until thickened. Next add vegetable broth and pureed zucchini in the saucepan. Cook for 20 minutes. Add milk last 5 minutes. Once you ladle in soup bowl add a dollop of sour cream and lightly sprinkle paprika.

We sprinkle crushed red pepper flakes for a little extra kick.

BLT 7 Layer Salad

Serves 4-6

- ☐ 12 oz. Romain, washed and chopped
- ☐ 2 large tomatoes, cleaned and diced small
- ☐ 1 lb. penne pasta, cooked and cooled
- ☐ 1 lb. sliced bacon, cooked and broken into bite size pieces
- ☐ ½ c. pickled onions
- ☐ 2 c. cheddar, shredded
- ☐ 1 c. carrots, shredded
- ☐ 1 c. celery, thinly sliced
- ☐ 1 c. Italian croutons
- ☐ 2 tsp. fresh chives, thinly chopped
- ☐ Dressing of choice

Layering begins with ½ each lettuce, pasta, veggies, cheese, bacon, dressing, then croutons. Top with chives and serve immediately. If serving later, omit the dressing and add dressing before serving. It can be chilled for 6 hours before serving.

Curry Chicken Salad

Serves 8

- ☐ 4 c. cooked chicken breast, cubed
- ☐ 1 c. mayo
- ☐ 1 c. Greek Yogurt, plain
- ☐ 1 tbs. Curry powder
- ☐ 1 c. chicken broth
- ☐ ¼ c. chutney
- ☐ 2 large celery ribs, diced
- ☐ ¼ c. scallions, diced
- ☐ ½ c. carrots, shredded
- ☐ 1 tsp. onion powder
- ☐ ¼ c. raisins
- ☐ 1 tsp. sugar
- ☐ 1 c. whole cashews, lightly toasted

Combine all ingredients in large bowl. Chill for 6-8 hours.

Never add mixture to warm chicken.

Italian
Pasta Salad

Serves 6

- ☐ 1 lb. rotini, cooked and cool rinsed
- ☐ 1 c. extra virgin olive oil
- ☐ ½ c. red wine vinegar
- ☐ ¼ c. pesto
- ☐ 1 tbs. sundried tomato paste
- ☐ ½ c. granulated sugar
- ☐ 1 garlic clove, minced
- ☐ 1 tsp. each salt, pepper, basil, oregano
- ☐ 1 c. each salami, pepperoni, and sweet ham (diced)
- ☐ 1 c. mozzarella, shredded
- ☐ 1 c. cherry tomatoes, halved
- ☐ 1 c. black or kalamata olives, sliced
- ☐ 1 c. celery, thinly sliced
- ☐ 1 c. multi-colored bell peppers, julienned
- ☐ ¼ c. banana peppers
- ☐ 1 c. garlic seasoned croutons

Combine vinegar, sugar, pesto, tomato paste, garlic and oil. Toss into the pasta, coating generously. Top with remaining toppings reserving croutons.

Croutons are best added when serving. Our daughter Courtney is such a help at family gatherings. She likes to make this dish with me. #blessed

Southern
Potato Salad

Serves 8

- ☐ 12 medium potatoes, peeled and cubed
- ☐ 2 eggs, boiled, peeled and cubed
- ☐ 1 c. mayo
- ☐ 1 c. Greek Yogurt, plain
- ☐ ½ c. sweet pickle relish
- ☐ 1 tbs. yellow mustard
- ☐ 2 tbs. Thousand Island dressing
- ☐ 1 tsp. each garlic powder, onion powder, paprika
- ☐ 2 large celery ribs, diced
- ☐ ¼ c. scallions, diced
- ☐ 2 tbs. parsley
- ☐ 2 tsp. sugar
- ☐ salt & pepper to taste

Peel and cube potatoes. Add potatoes to salted boiling water. Boil until tender about 5-8 minutes. Don't let potatoes become mushy. Check after 5 minutes by using a fork. Combine all the remaining ingredients together in a large bowl while the potatoes are boiling. Rinse potatoes in cold water until potatoes are room temp. Drain well and place in refrigerator for 15 minutes. Add wet mixture to cooled potatoes folding together gently. Chill for 30 minutes to an hour before serving. Top with Paprika and fresh or dried parsley.

Apple, Bacon, and Smoked Gouda Salad

Serves 4-6

- ☐ 2 Granny Smith or Gala apples, large, thinly sliced
- ☐ 2 tbs. fresh lemon juice
- ☐ 12 oz. Romain, Arugula, Baby Spinach mix
- ☐ 4 bacon slices, cooked and crumbled
- ☐ 2 tbs. pickled onions
- ☐ 2 c. Smoked Gouda, shredded
- ☐ 1 c. sliced sweet grapes
- ☐ 1 c. celery, thinly sliced
- ☐ 1 tsp. parsley flakes
- ☐ 1 c. dried cranberries
- ☐ Dressing of choice

Pour lemon juice over apples and coat evenly. Combine all ingredients except pickled onions and bacon crumbles. Reserve those as salad toppings. Toss with your favorite dressing at time of serving. You can make ahead and held in the refrigerator 8 hours without dressing.

*Add 3 c. rotisserie chicken, diced for extra protein.

*For a burst of flavors, use strawberry balsamic with olive oil for the dressing. This salad leaves plenty of room to add other favorite veggies or fruit such as fresh sliced strawberries or pomegranates. My adorable niece (Alessandra) loves this salad. For years, we have been swapping yummy recipes back and forth.

Southern
Chicken Salad

Serves 8

- [ ] 4 c. cooked chicken breast, cubed or shredded small pieces
- [ ] 1 c. mayo
- [ ] 1 c. Greek Yogurt, plain
- [ ] 1 tsp. Dijon mustard
- [ ] 1 tsp. lemon juice
- [ ] 1 tbs. granulated sugar
- [ ] ½ tsp. turmeric, salt, and tsp. tarragon (dried)
- [ ] 1 tsp. onion powder, garlic powder, granulated sugar
- [ ] 1 c. purple or red seedless grapes, quartered
- [ ] ¾ c. Craisins, dried cranberries
- [ ] 1 celery rib, diced small bits
- [ ] ¼ c. sweet pickle relish

Combine all ingredients to the chilled chicken. Chill for 6-8 hours.

*When cooking your chicken in salted water, add 1 Bay leaf, 1 small onion, and 1 celery rib. This makes a huge difference in taste.
OPTIONAL add lightly toasted and crushed pecans
*Always best served on a bed of lettuce and fresh croissant. My dear friend Michelle loves this recipe. I make extra to share with her when our schedules align.

Corn and Tomato Salad

Serves 4-6

- ☐ 2 c. cooked corn, fresh or frozen
- ☐ ½ c. red onions, minced
- ☐ 1 pint cherry tomatoes, halved

Dressing:

- ☐ 1 lime, zested and juiced
- ☐ 2 tbs. olive oil
- ☐ ¼ c. cilantro, finely chopped
- ☐ ¼ tsp. kosher salt & pepper
- ☐ 1 tsp. garlic and onion powder
- ☐ ½ tsp. ground cummin

Combine all dressing ingredients. Next combine corn, tomatoes and onions. Pour dressing over corn mixture. Refrigerate up to 4 hours.

*My mom makes this salad with 1 chopped avocado. It is fabulous to have it as a light appetizer or a side to a meal. Recommend this salad with tortilla chips.

*If using fresh corn off the cob, boil for a minimum of (5) five minutes.

4-6 ears yields 2 cups

Greek Veggie Pasta Salad

Serves 12

- ☐ 2 lb. rotini, cooked and rinsed in cool water
- ☐ 1 c. Greek yogurt
- ☐ 16 oz. Tzatziki
- ☐ 1 c. feta cheese crumbles
- ☐ 1 c. vegetable broth
- ☐ 1 c. mozzarella, shredded
- ☐ 1 c. carrots, minced
- ☐ 1 c. celery, thinly sliced
- ☐ 1 c. cucumbers, diced
- ☐ ¼ c. banana peppers, diced
- ☐ ¼ c. sweet peppers, julienne cut
- ☐ 2 tbs. kalamata olives, sliced in half
- ☐ 2 tbs. pickled red sweet onions
- ☐ 2 tbs. fresh dill, chopped
- ☐ 1 tsp. each dried parsley, basil, oregano, thyme

Combine all wet ingredients then toss with seasonings, cheese and pasta in a large bowl. Layer top with Tzatziki, then sprinkle with veggies for a burst of color and flavors.

Entrees & Sides

Au Jus Beef Stroganoff

Serves 4

- ☐ 1 lb. egg noodles, cooked al dente and ran under cold water
- ☐ 1 can cream of mushroom
- ☐ 1 package dry Au Jus seasoning
- ☐ 3 tbs. butter
- ☐ 2 tbs. olive oil
- ☐ ½ lb. mushrooms, sliced
- ☐ ½ c. finely chopped onions
- ☐ 1 ½ lbs. ground beef, browned and drained
- ☐ 1 tsp. salt
- ☐ 1 tsp. Dijon mustard
- ☐ 2 tsp. Worcestershire sauce
- ☐ ½ tsp. paprika and black pepper
- ☐ 1 c. sour cream
- ☐ 1 c. beef broth or water
- ☐ Parsley to garnish

Combine all ingredients and serve over egg noodles. Garnish with Parsley. Cover and bake in preheated 350 oven for 40 minutes.

Cook the egg noodles 3 minutes less than the package instructions.

Honey Baked Ham with Pineapple

Serves 12

- [ ] 6 lb. Baked Ham (thoroughly cooked, not spiral)
- [ ] 1 c. Honey (Wildflower is most popular and affordable)
- [ ] 4 tbs. Brown Sugar
- [ ] 7.5 oz sliced pineapple in natural syrup
- [ ] 1 jar of cherries in their juice

Preheat over 350. Mix all ingredients except pineapple slices and cherries. Pour over ham. Grease 9x13x2 pan. Before baking ham, add pineapple rings and juice on top of ham. Use toothpicks and pin the cherries inside pineapple rings. Bake 350 for 2 hours.

I like to add cloves for a hint of spice and tartness.

Italian
Ziti Bake

Serves 6

- ☐ 1 lb. Italian Mild sausage
- ☐ 1 large can Marzano Whole Tomatoes
- ☐ 1 small can of Stewed Tomatoes
- ☐ 4 medium ripe tomatoes (diced)
- ☐ 1 c. grated parmesan
- ☐ 2 c. shredded mozzarella cheese
- ☐ 1 c. beef broth
- ☐ 1 tbs. minced garlic
- ☐ ½ tsp. each salt and pepper
- ☐ 1 tsp. onion powder, pepper, oregano. basil
- ☐ 1 package of Penne pasta (or other tubular pasta)
- ☐ 1 c. of ricotta cheese
- ☐ 1 egg

Boil pasta according to al dente instructions. Mix all cheese and egg, set aside. Sautee the sausage, drain on paper towel. Place all tomatoes and herbs in a large sauce pot, bring to a boil then reduce heat to med-low for 20 minutes. Use an immersion blender or blender to blend tomatoes and herbs.
Add meat to sauce. Spead cheese blend over the pasta in a 10x13 baking dish. Cover with sauce. Bake at 400 for 30 minutes.

*Always a nice presentation to add fresh basil or parsley on top before serving.

Breakfast Casserole

Serves 6

- ☐ 18 oz. fresh ground breakfast sausage, browned, drained, crumbled
- ☐ 6 slices of cooked bacon, chopped
- ☐ 8 eggs
- ☐ 1 c. milk
- ☐ 1 can biscuits (any brand, Buttermilk preferred)
- ☐ 1 medium onion, chopped, slightly sauteed
- ☐ 2 c. shredded cheddar cheese
- ☐ ½ stick of butter, melted

Coat 13x9 pan with cooking spray or butter. Flatten biscuits to cover bottom of pan. Bake for 5 minutes in a preheated 350 degrees oven. Whisk eggs, add onions, sausage, and mix well. Pour into pan on top of pre-baked biscuits. Sprinkle with cheese and bacon. Pour butter over the top.
Bake 350 for 40 minutes

Spice it up! Omit diced onions, add a can of drained Rotel, sauteed mushrooms and minced jalapenos.

Broccoli Rice Casserole

Serves 8

- ☐ 1 small onion (minced)
- ☐ ½ stick of butter
- ☐ ¼ tsp. cayenne powder
- ☐ 10 oz. cream of mushroom
- ☐ ½ c. flour
- ☐ 3 c. whole milk
- ☐ 4 oz. cream cheese
- ☐ ¼ c. Parmesan cheese
- ☐ 1 tsp. each paprika and mustard powder
- ☐ 1 small block of Velveeta or processed cheese block
- ☐ 1 head of broccoli, separate into small florets
- ☐ 1 small jar pimentos, diced
- ☐ 8 slices of bacon, cooked and crumbled
- ☐ 8 c. cooked long white grain rice

Sauté onions in butter. Add flour, cayenne, and mustard powder to onions stirring for 2 minutes. Add milk, cream cheese, parmesan, cream of mushroom soup, paprika, 1 c. cheddar cheese, and Velveeta stirring for 5 minutes. Add broccoli florets, and pimentos. Mixture should be slightly thick. In a sprayed baking dish, layer rice then broccoli cheese mixture, repeating two times. Top with 1 c. shredded cheddar and crumbled bacon. Cover and bake 350 degrees for 25 minutes, then uncover for 20 minutes.

Mexican Burrito Pie

Serves 6

- [ ] 2 lbs. ground beef, browned, drained
- [ ] 12 medium flour tortilla shells
- [ ] 1 can Rotel, drained
- [ ] 10 oz. cream of mushroom soup
- [ ] 24 oz. enchilada sauce
- [ ] 1 tsp. garlic, fresh grated or jar
- [ ] 1 large onion and bell pepper, chopped
- [ ] 4 c. shredded cheddar cheese
- [ ] ½ stick of butter, to sauté the veggies in
- [ ] 2 tsp. cumin
- [ ] 1 tbs. paprika
- [ ] 2 tbs. cilantro

Coat 13x9 glass or non-stick pan with spray or butter. Sautee chopped veggies for 5 minutes in 2 tbs. of butter. Combine beef, sauteed veggies, soup, seasonings, 12 oz. enchilada sauce and Rotel. Cover the bottom of pan with tortilla shells. Spread beef mixture over the flour shells, sprinkle 2 c. cheese, next top cheese with 12 oz. enchilada sauce. Repeat layering process. Cover with remaining enchilada sauce. Cover and bake 375 degrees for 55 minutes. Uncover the last 5 minutes.

My big brother Jim loves this dish with diced Jalapenos baked on top.

Italian Tomato Sandwich

Serves 4

- [ ] 8 slices of your choice of bread
- [ ] 2 large Farmhouse or Garden Tomatoes, sliced
- [ ] 2 tbs. of Pesto Mayo
- [ ] 8 thick slices of Mozzarella
- [ ] 8 large fresh Basil leaves
- [ ] 4 small tomatoes, sliced small
- [ ] 1 tsp. onion powder
- [ ] ½ tsp. each of fresh black pepper and sea salt
- [ ] 2 tbs. each balsamic vinegar and olive oil

Toast your bread. Allow toast to cool then add *pesto mayo and layer the tomatoes and cheese. Top with fresh basil, drizzles of your favorite balsamic vinegar and olive oil, salt and pepper.

*You can find the *Pesto Mayo recipe located in the Canning & Sauces chapter.

*These are perfect, quick and simple to have after a summer day in the sun.

Butternut Sausage Tortellini Casserole

Serves 6

- ☐ 1 lb. tortellini cheese pasta
- ☐ 1 lb. Italian sausage, browned and drained
- ☐ 1 whole butternut squash, peeled and cubed 1in.
- ☐ 1 small onion, minced
- ☐ 1 tbs. garlic, minced
- ☐ 8 oz. chicken broth
- ☐ 1 c. ricotta cheese
- ☐ 1 can cream of chicken
- ☐ 1 can cream of golden mushroom
- ☐ 1 c. melted butter
- ☐ 1 tsp. each thyme, Italian seasonings, salt, and pepper
- ☐ 2 tbs. parsley flakes, topping decor
- ☐ 1 c. Italian breadcrumbs

Preheat oven to 375 degrees. Prepare to roast small cubed squash (discarding the seeds) sprinkle with olive oil salt and pepper to taste. Roast for 15 mins. Combine all ingredients (reserving breadcrumbs for topping and parsley) into 9x13 baking dish. Top with breadcrumbs and cover with foil. Bake for 45 minutes. Top with parsley before serving.

This is one of many dishes which remind me of my sweet niece, Katie. She is also very creative in the kitchen with savory and delicious dishes.

Cheeseburger Meatloaf

Serves 8

- ☐ 2 lbs. ground beef
- ☐ 1 can cream mushroom soup
- ☐ 2 c. ketchup
- ☐ 1 tbs. yellow mustard
- ☐ ½ c. fine breadcrumbs
- ☐ 1 egg, slightly beaten
- ☐ 4 slices of bread
- ☐ ½ tsp. salt
- ☐ 1 tsp. paprika, pepper, garlic powder
- ☐ ½ c. onion, minced
- ☐ ¼ c. water
- ☐ 1 tbs. Worcestershire sauce
- ☐ hot sauce, to taste

Preheat over 350. Mix all ingredients except bread slices and 1 c. ketchup. Place the bread slices on bottom of the pan then form mixture into the loaf pan. Cover meatloaf with the ketchup. Bake 375 for 45 minutes.

I like to add sliced "tamed" pickled jalapenos in mixture. The brine from the pickled Jalapenos gives it a different taste. The "tamed" jalapenos are not hot, milder.
This is fabulous served with dill pickles. waffle fries or onion rings.

Chicken and Dumplings

Serves 8

Broth:

- [ ] 1 whole chicken, cut into pieces
- [ ] 4 c. each chicken broth and vegetable broth
- [ ] 1 can cream of chicken soup
- [ ] ½ tsp. each poultry seasoning, thyme, salt and pepper
- [ ] 2 bay leaves (whole)

Dumplings:

- [ ] 1 ½ c. *AP flour (plus 1 cup for dusting)
- [ ] 1/3 c. shortening
- [ ] ½ tsp. baking powder
- [ ] ½ tsp. salt
- [ ] ¾ c. milk
- [ ] 4 tbs. cornstarch

Combine ingredients listed under broth and bring to a boil. Simmer on low boil for 40 minutes. Remove chicken, debone, remove skin and cut into small pieces. Combine dumplings ingredients except milk and cornstarch mixing well with fork. Add small amounts of milk until combined well. Add flour to the working surface. Knead a few times until the dough is smooth. Cut dough in 1x1 ½ inch piece strips. Add chicken and dumplings to the broth. Do Not Stir. Boil for 15 minutes. Mix 4 tbs. of cornstarch to 4 tbs. of cold water and add to broth. Blend until smooth, then add to broth to thicken if needed. Continue boiling for another 5 minutes. Remove bay leaves.

Chicken and Cornbread Casserole

Serves 8

- ☐ ¾ c. whole milk
- ☐ 1 can cream corn
- ☐ 1 can cream of chicken soup
- ☐ 1 can cream of mushroom soup
- ☐ 1 box jiffy corn mix
- ☐ 2 c. shredded cheese
- ☐ 1 c. sour cream
- ☐ 1 small bag of frozen carrots and peas (defrosted)
- ☐ 1 egg
- ☐ 1 tsp. each salt & pepper
- ☐ 1 tbs. garlic powder
- ☐ 1 tsp. Worchester sauce
- ☐ 1 rotisserie chicken, pulled and chopped

Combine milk, cheese, soups, seasonings, Worchester, veggies and chicken. Pour that mixture into a greased baking dish. Mix corn, box of jiffy, sour cream, egg, and 2 tbs. of melted butter. Pour cornbread mixture on top of chicken mixture. Bake on 400 degrees uncovered for 35 minutes, covered for 10 minutes to stop from burning cornbread crust.

This recipe reminds me of chicken pot pie except the crust is cornbread. Perfect in the Fall to have this warm dish.

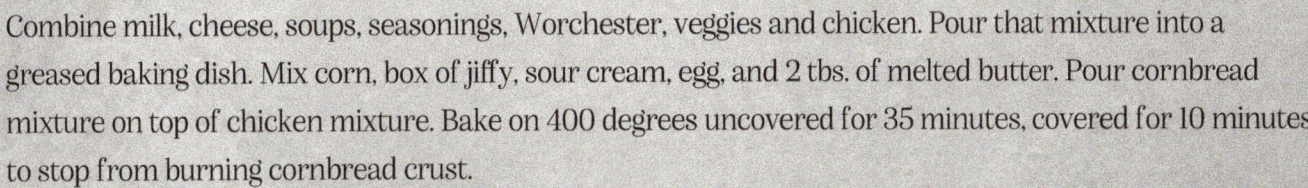

Chicken Enchiladas

Serves 8

- ☐ 4 chicken breasts or 8 chicken thighs, boneless
- ☐ 8 x-large flour tortilla shells
- ☐ 20 oz. enchilada sauce, red
- ☐ 1 package fajita seasoning
- ☐ 1 package ranch dip seasoning
- ☐ 4 c. shredded cheddar cheese
- ☐ 1 c. chicken broth
- ☐ 1 can Rotel, drained
- ☐ 1 tbs. Franks hot sauce
- ☐ ¼ stick of butter
- ☐ 1 tsp. each cumin, onion powder, pepper
- ☐ 1 tsp. granulated onion
- ☐ 1 tsp. fresh garlic
- ☐ 12 medium soft flour shells
- ☐ 1 tbs. fresh chopped cilantro
- ☐ 4 oz. cream cheese

Place all ingredients in crockpot except tortilla shells and shredded cheese. Cook on high for 3 hours. Lightly cover bottom of 10x13 baking dish with half of the enchilada sauce. Roll chicken mixture in shells. Top with remaining enchilada sauce and cheese. Bake covered 350 degrees 30 minutes, then uncovered 10 minutes.

Chicken
Pot Pie

Serves 6

- ☐ 4 c. cooked or rotisserie chicken, shredded
- ☐ 1 can cream mushroom and cream of chicken soup
- ☐ 1 can buttermilk biscuits
- ☐ 2 c. chicken broth
- ☐ 1 c. half and half or milk (not evaporated)
- ☐ 4 tbs. *AP (all purpose) flour
- ☐ 5 tbs. butter
- ☐ ¼ c. milk
- ☐ ½ small onion, diced
- ☐ 2 celery stalks, diced
- ☐ 2 medium potatoes, small cubes then boiled for 5 minutes
- ☐ 1 small bag of frozen carrots and peas
- ☐ 1 tsp. each poultry seasoning, sea salt, pepper, onion powder, garlic powder, thyme, parsley

Sautee butter in pan add onions and celery. Slowly adding AP flour. Whisk constantly at a med high temp. Once the roux is thick add broth and milk. Continue to whisk until bubbly. Add water until it is thin and smooth. Everything now goes into the pot except the biscuits. Pour into a greased 10x13 baking pan. Top with flaked biscuits pulled in half the original thickness. Bake on 400 degrees covered for 45-50 minutes, uncover for an additional 10 minutes.

Cowboy Tater-Tot Casserole

Serves 6-8

- ☐ 1 lb. hamburger, cooked, drained
- ☐ 1 lb. tater tots, frozen
- ☐ 2 c. cheddar cheese, shredded
- ☐ 1 sweet onion, medium, diced
- ☐ 1 can condensed mushroom soup
- ☐ 1 cup sour cream
- ☐ 1 tsp. salt
- ☐ ½ c. mushroom, sliced
- ☐ ½ c. green onions, diced
- ☐ 1 can cheddar cheese soup
- ☐ ¼ tsp. pepper
- ☐ 1 tsp. each garlic powder and onion powder
- ☐ 1 tsp. Worcestershire
- ☐ 1 tsp. Dijon mustard

Grease 9x13x2 pan. Reserve half tater-tots, cheddar cheese, and green onions aside to top casserole. Next layer the bottom of pan with Tater-Tots with 1 cup of cheese on top. Combine remaining ingredients. Fill pan, then top casserole with reserved half of tater-tots. Preheat, cover and Bake 350 for 1 hour. Pull casserole from oven, then top with the last cup of cheddar cheese and green onions.

Elaine's Pepper Steak with Rice

Serves 6

- [ ] 3 c. rice, cooked
- [ ] 1 lb. tender steak, cubed
- [ ] 1 tbs. paprika
- [ ] 2 tbs. butter
- [ ] 2 c. beef broth
- [ ] 2 cloves garlic, minced
- [ ] 1 ½ small green onion, sliced thinly
- [ ] 2 green peppers, strips
- [ ] 2 tbs. cornstarch
- [ ] ¼ c. each soy and water
- [ ] 1 large tomato, diced
- [ ] 2 tsp. Worcestershire sauce
- [ ] 1 tsp. each salt, black pepper, onion powder, paprika

Marinate steak with dry seasonings and Worcestershire for 1 hour. Add butter to hot skillet and brown meat for 5 minutes, add garlic and broth. Cover and simmer for 30 minutes. Add onions and peppers, cook additional 5 minutes covered. Blend water, soy and cornstarch, then stir into meat mixture. Cook stirring until thickened (about 2 minutes). Add tomatoes at the very end, stirring gently. Serve over a bed of fluffy rice.

My late mother-in-law, (Elaine) made this amazing dish. She kept it simple, and it is my father-in-law's favorite dish.

Garlic Chicken and Rice

Serves 4

- ☐ 2 c. rotisserie chicken, diced
- ☐ 1 can cream of chicken soup
- ☐ 1 tbs. onion, diced
- ☐ 2 tsp. garlic, minced
- ☐ 2 c. cooked rice
- ☐ 1 tsp. parsley flakes
- ☐ 1 tsp. ground mustard
- ☐ 1 c. chicken broth
- ☐ 1 tbs. lemon juice
- ☐ ½ stick butter
- ☐ 1 c. celery, diced
- ☐ Salt & pepper to taste
- ☐ 2 tbs. sour cream
- ☐ 1 c. corn flakes, crushed

Preheat oven 375. Pour all ingredients except corn flakes into a 9x9 baking dish. Melt butter in saucepan and combine with cornflakes. Pour cornflakes on top of dish, cover and bake 30 minutes, uncover last 10 minutes.

Ground Turkey Stir Fry

Serves 6

- ☐ 2 lb. ground turkey, browned and drained
- ☐ 4 c. steamed rice
- ☐ 1 small onion, diced
- ☐ 2 c. fresh white mushrooms, sliced thin
- ☐ 2 tsp. garlic, minced
- ☐ 1 tbs. ginger, minced
- ☐ 1 tbs. lime juice
- ☐ ½ stick butter
- ☐ ¼ c. sodium free soy
- ☐ 1 c. each celery and red pepper, diced and carrots, shredded
- ☐ 1 small zucchini, diced
- ☐ 1 can water chestnuts, drained and julienned
- ☐ 1 small bunch of Bok Choy, thin sliced
- ☐ 1 c. scallions, sliced thin
- ☐ salt & pepper to taste

Melt butter in saucepan and combine all vegetables reserving the scallions in to pan. Sautee for 10 minutes uncovered; then additional 20 minutes covered. Uncover and toss in ground turkey, soy and scallions. Serve over rice or Asian noodles of preference.

This is our son's favorite dish! He will top his with a few scrambled eggs and sweet chili sauce.

Honey Garlic Shrimp

Serves 4

- ☐ 2 lbs. 20 count shrimp, raw not frozen
- ☐ 1 tbs. white onion, diced
- ☐ 1 tbs. brown sugar
- ☐ ½ c. honey
- ☐ 2 tsp. garlic, minced
- ☐ 1 tsp. parsley flakes, thyme, oregano
- ☐ 1 c. chicken broth
- ☐ 1 tbs. lime juice
- ☐ ½ stick butter
- ☐ 2 scallions, thinly sliced
- ☐ Salt & pepper to taste

Preheat oven 375. Melt butter in large skillet on medium-high. Add white onions and garlic sauté for 4 minutes. Next add chicken broth, sugar, honey, lime juice, and seasonings. Continue stirring for an additional 5 minutes. Pour all ingredients into a 9x13 baking dish. Cover and bake for 20 minutes. Top with freshly cut scallions.

Pairs nicely with buttered rice or over a bed of angel hair pasta.

Crockpot Italian Sausage and Tortellini

Serves 6

- ☐ 38 oz. cheese filled tortellini
- ☐ 28 oz. crushed tomatoes
- ☐ 28 oz. tomato sauce
- ☐ 2 lbs. Italian sausage, mild
- ☐ 1 large red onion, minced
- ☐ 4 garlic cloves, minced
- ☐ 1 tbs. sundried tomatoes, paste
- ☐ 1 tsp. each thyme, oregano, basil, salt, and pepper
- ☐ 2 tbs. granulated sugar
- ☐ 2 Tbsp. parsley flakes
- ☐ ½ tsp. red pepper flakes
- ☐ 1 c. half & half
- ☐ 1 c. parmesan cheese

Brown the sausage, garlic, and onions together, Drain sausage and place in slow cooker. Place frozen tortellini on top of meat. Next blend all seasonings with tomatoes and sugar then pour on top of tortellini. Do not stir, this should be layered. Cook on high for 2 hours or low for 4 hours. Add half & half last 15 minutes. Top with parmesan cheese before serving.

Pairs well with a nice garden salad and garlic bread. My dear late friend Jennie loved this dish!!

Lemon Shrimp and Spinach

Serves 4

- ☐ 2 lb. fresh shrimp
- ☐ 4 garlic cloves, minced
- ☐ 2 tbs. olive oil
- ☐ 1 c. chicken broth
- ☐ ½ c. melted butter
- ☐ 2 tsp. lemon zest
- ☐ 3 tbs. fresh lemon juice
- ☐ 1/2 tsp. crushed red pepper flakes
- ☐ 8 oz. fresh baby spinach
- ☐ 2 tbs. parsley flakes
- ☐ salt and pepper to taste

Peel and clean shrimp. Sauté shrimp and garlic in oi for 5 minutes on medium-high. Once the shrimp turns pink, remove the shrimp then add broth, lemon juice and zest. Loosen the particles from the bottom of pan cooking 4 minutes. Add the spinach and cook for 2 minutes or until wilted. Sprinkle with seasonings.

My sissy loves this with her favorite pasta and garlic bread.

Loaded Butternut Squash Chicken Cordon Bleu

Serves 4

- ☐ 2 large Butternut Squash, discard seeds
- ☐ 1 egg, beaten
- ☐ 2 tbs. Dijon mustard
- ☐ 1 green onion, sliced
- ☐ 2 c. smoked ham, diced
- ☐ 2 c. rotisserie chicken, diced
- ☐ 1 lb. Swiss cheese, shredded or diced small
- ☐ 1 tsp. parsley
- ☐ 2 tbs. Olive Oil
- ☐ 1 c. plain breadcrumbs

Brush squash in olive oil, cover with foil and roast for 60-90 minutes on 375, until tender. Scoop out most of the squash, not all the way to the skin. Leave 1 inch thickness on the bottom. Mash the squash scooped out. Add salt, pepper, cheese, ham, chicken, mustard and egg. Mix all well and fill in squash shells. Top with breadcrumbs. Bake covered 425 for 15 minutes. Uncover and bake additional 5 minutes. Let cool for 10 minutes before serving. Sprinkle with green onion.

Recent dish that our family fell in love with. Must try in the Fall or Winter.

Mediterranean Eggplant and Zucchini

Serves 6

- ☐ 1 large Eggplant, diced
- ☐ 1 large Zucchini, diced
- ☐ 1 lb. penne or rotini pasta, cooked and drained
- ☐ 1 small onion, diced
- ☐ 1 tsp. garlic, minced
- ☐ 1 celery stalk, diced
- ☐ 1 red pepper, chopped
- ☐ 2 tbs. mixed Italian seasonings (oregano, basil, thyme)
- ☐ 1 c. white wine
- ☐ 2 c. tomato puree
- ☐ 2 c. vegetable broth
- ☐ 2 tbs. Olive Oil
- ☐ ½ tsp. red pepper flakes
- ☐ 1 c. Parmesan, shredded
- ☐ ½ c. Half & Half
- ☐ salt & pepper to taste

Combine zucchini and eggplant lightly toss in olive oil and roast for 20 minutes on 400. Add onion, garlic, celery, red pepper, and seasonings in olive oil for 5 minutes over med-high heat. Add white wine to pan for an additional 4 minutes. Lastly add the tomato puree, broth with cheese and milk, simmer for another 10 minutes. Use immersion blender until smooth. Bring all together, plate the pasta, top with red sauce then eggplant and zucchini.

Mexican Beef Cornbread Casserole

Serves 8-12

- ☐ 2 lbs. cooked ground beef
- ☐ 8 oz. sour cream
- ☐ 2 packages Jiffy Cornbread mix
- ☐ 2 cans of sweet, creamed corn
- ☐ 4 c. cheddar cheese, shredded
- ☐ ½ c. melted butter
- ☐ 2 tsp. cumin
- ☐ 1 large egg
- ☐ 1 tbs. white sugar
- ☐ ½ sweet onion, slightly sautéed
- ☐ 1 can Rotel, drained

Coat 11x13 non-stick pan or a buttered cast iron skillet. Combine jiffy mix, sour cream, corn, cumin, sugar, and egg in a small bowl. Next combine meat, 2 c. cheese, Rotel, and onion. Pour into casserole dish, cover and bake in preheated 375 oven for 30 minutes. Uncover, add the remaining 2 cups of cheese continue baking uncovered an additional 10 minutes.

Optional to top with fresh sour cream, fresh cilantro and pickled jalapenos.

Bow-Tie Pasta with Smoked Turkey Sausage

Serves 6

- ☐ 1 lb. farfalle pasta
- ☐ 1 lb. Smoked Turkey Sausage
- ☐ 1 small onion, minced
- ☐ 4 garlic cloves, minced
- ☐ ¼ c. balsamic vinegar
- ☐ 16 oz. chicken broth
- ☐ 1 c. melted butter
- ☐ 8 oz. fresh spinach or kale
- ☐ 2 Tbsp. sundried tomatoes, diced
- ☐ 1 tsp. each thyme, Italian seasonings, salt, and pepper
- ☐ 2 Tbsp. parsley flakes

Prepare pasta according to directions. Heat thin slices of sausage for 8 minutes, add onions and seasonings continue cooking additional 5 minutes on medium-high. Next add garlic, vinegar and broth. Lastly, add fresh spinach or kale and toss in the pasta. Sprinkle with feta.

*I bring this dish to another level with fresh squeezed lemon juice.

Pierogi Casserole

Serves 4-6

- ☐ 2 tbs. EVO (extra virgin olive oil)
- ☐ 2 lb. favorite frozen Pierogies
- ☐ 1 can cheddar cheese or cream of mushroom soup
- ☐ 8 oz. cheddar cheese, shredded
- ☐ 8 oz. ricotta cheese
- ☐ 8 oz. sour cream
- ☐ 1 small onion, thinly sliced
- ☐ 1 lb. smoked kielbasa, sliced thin
- ☐ 1 tsp. each black pepper, garlic powder, onion powder, paprika
- ☐ 1 tsp. Kosher Salt to taste
- ☐   2 scallions, thinly sliced for topping

Mix olive oil, onion, seasonings and sauté with sausage in pan. In a separate bowl combine remaining ingredients reserving scallions for toppings. Layer Cheese, then Sausage and Pierogies. Bake covered 350 for 40 minutes.

Pairs well with a side of sautéed cabbage and pepper sauce.

Easy Ham & Cheese Quiche

Serves 4

- ☐ 1 pie crust, unbaked
- ☐ 6 large eggs
- ☐ 1 c. cheddar cheese, shredded
- ☐ 1 c. Swiss cheese, shredded
- ☐ ¾ c. half & half
- ☐ ¾ tsp. salt
- ☐ ¼ tsp. black pepper
- ☐ 1 c. sweet deli ham, chopped
- ☐ ½ small onion, sliced thin
- ☐ 2 slices bacon, cut into inch pieces
- ☐ 3 tbs. butter, unsalted

Cook bacon and onions. Preheat oven to 375 degrees. Whisk together eggs, milk salt and pepper. Add ham, cheese, bacon, butter and onion mix into 9 in. pie crust. Sprinkle remaining cheese on top. Bake for 35-40 minutes until the center is completely set. Allow it to cool for 30 minutes.

Grew up having quiches with all different varieties. Favorite has thin sliced tomatoes on top with ham and diced jalapenos.

Rueben Casserole

Serves 4

- ☐ 2 lbs. corned beef, shaved
- ☐ 1 loaf of Rye bread, toasted and medium crumbles
- ☐ 16 oz. sauerkraut, drained
- ☐ 1 tsp. each garlic powder, onion powder
- ☐ 4 c. Swiss cheese, shredded
- ☐ 8 slices of smoked provolone
- ☐ 1 c. Thousand Island dressing
- ☐ 2 tsp. Dijon mustard
- ☐ ½ c. mayo
- ☐ ½ c. melted butter
- ☐ 2 tsp. cumin

Coat glass or non-stick pan with cooking spray or additional butter. Layer bottom with Rye bread crumbles, cover with sauerkraut. Combine mayo, mustard, and Thousand Island dressing. Spread half dressing over the kraut. Layer down provolone and 2 c. Swiss cheese over kraut then layer with deli corned beef. Cover the last of the dressing over the corned beef. Cover with remaining bread and cheese then drizzle butter over the casserole. Bake in preheated 350 oven for 40 minutes. Uncover and bake an additional 10 minutes.

I have substituted 1 sauteed onion and 1 small head of cabbage ribbons, drained. In leu of the sauerkraut. I like both ways.
Pairs well with buttered rice.

Penne and Roasted Shrimp

Serves 8

- ☐ 2 lbs. (36 count) shrimp
- ☐ ½ stick of butter, melted
- ☐ ¼ tsp. cayenne powder
- ☐ 3 tbs. olive oil
- ☐ 1 tsp. each paprika and black pepper
- ☐ 2 tsp. Old Bay
- ☐ ½ c. each scallion, parsley, and dill
- ☐ ½ red onion, diced
- ☐ 2 lemons, juiced
- ☐ 1 lb. penne, cooked and drained

In a large mixing bowl, toss shrimp, olive oil, melted butter, cayenne, paprika, pepper and Old Bay seasoning. Let shrimp marinade for 10 minutes then place on parchment paper lined baking sheet. Roast shrimp on 400 degrees in a preheated oven for 6 minutes each side. Rest shrimp for 10 minutes. Toss with the scallions, parsley, dill, red onions, lemons, and shrimp into the cooled penne pasta.

I love this dish which reminds me of my dear friend Katie in Ohio. We loved cooking together and for other friends. Katie is my sister from another mother who helped me through some very rough patches in my life. #forever #grateful

Shrimp & Grits

Serves 8

- ☐ 4 c. grits
- ☐ 2 c. cheddar cheese and smoked gouda cheese, shredded
- ☐ 4 oz. cream cheese, softened
- ☐ 1 tsp. each nutmeg and white pepper
- ☐ 2 lb. medium shrimp, peeled and deveined
- ☐ 1 tbs. Old Bay seasoning
- ☐ 12 slices of bacon
- ☐ 1 box chicken broth
- ☐ ½ stick of butter
- ☐ 4 tsp. lemon juice
- ☐ 2 tbs. chopped parsley
- ☐ 2 garlic cloves, minced
- ☐ 2 c. mushrooms, thinly sliced
- ☐ 1 tsp. hot sauce

Prepare grits based on directions omitting water and using the chicken broth. Add butter, cheese, cream cheese and all seasonings. Keep on low stirring frequently. Peel and clean shrimp. Pat dry. Crisp bacon in hot skillet. Crumble bacon once cooled. Reserve the bacon renderings. Sauté shrimp, hot sauce, lemon juice, onions, garlic, and mushrooms in bacon renderings. Serve grits in large bowl add shrimp mixture on top of grits. Décor with bacon crumbles and parsley and remaining bacon renderings.

Stuffed Chicken with Sausage Stuffing

Serves 8

- ☐ 1 c. sage or country sausage, cooked, drained
- ☐ 4 large chicken breast, split open to allow stuffing
- ☐ 2 c. cornbread stuffing mix
- ☐ 2 c. bread stuffing mix
- ☐ 2 c. chicken broth, hot
- ☐ 1 c. water
- ☐ 4 tbs. butter, melted
- ☐ 1 tbs. lemon juice (fresh squeezed)
- ☐ 2 stalks of celery, diced
- ☐ ¼ onion, diced
- ☐ 1 tbs. olive oil
- ☐ 1 tsp. each onion powder, garlic powder, paprika, sugar

Sauté onions, celery in olive oil for 5 minutes. Add seasonings to the saucepan for the last minute. In a large bowl, add onion and celery mix to both stuffing, chicken broth, melted butter, lemon juice, and sausage. This should be dry to moist, not wet. Use the reserved water to add until you are satisfied with your consistency. Stuff chicken breast and place in baking dish. Cover and bake at 375 degrees for 30 minutes. Uncover and bake an additional 10 minutes. Chicken should not be pink.

For additional seasonings, add a touch of Cajun seasoning with minced jalapenos.

Stuffed
Bell Peppers

Serves 4

- ☐ 4 large bell peppers
- ☐ 1 small onion, chopped
- ☐ 2 lb. hamburger meat, lightly cooked
- ☐ 2 c. white rice, steamed
- ☐ ½ stick butter, melted
- ☐ 1 tsp. Worchester Sauce
- ☐ 1 can cream of mushroom
- ☐ 1 can fire roasted tomatoes, drained
- ☐ 1 can sweet whole kernel corn, drained
- ☐ 1 c. Italian breadcrumbs
- ☐ 1 c. cheddar jack cheese, shredded
- ☐ 1 c. provolone cheese, shredded
- ☐ Salt/Pepper to taste

Clean, remove tops, seeds and ribs from peppers (keeping them whole). Cook hamburger meat and onions together, drain well. Combine all ingredients, reserving the breadcrumbs and ¼ c. of provolone cheese. Stuff the mixture into the peppers. Cover generously with breadcrumbs. Place in a greased baking dish cover with aluminum foil. Bake 375 degrees for 35 minutes. Before serving, top with the remaining cheese.

Use turkey meat if you would like a healthier meat alternative.

Tex-Mex
Taco Burgers

Serves 4

- ☐ 1 lb. ground beef, browned, drained
- ☐ 1 package of Taco seasoning
- ☐ 1 c. taco sauce (no chunks)
- ☐ 1 c. cheddar cheese, shredded
- ☐ 1 c. Mexican cheese, shredded
- ☐ ½ head of iceberg lettuce, shredded thinly
- ☐ 1 tbs. onion, minced
- ☐ ½ stick butter
- ☐ 1 large tomato, diced
- ☐ ½ tsp. each cumin, granulated garlic, granulated onion
- ☐ salt & pepper to taste
- ☐ 4 hamburger buns

Preheat skillet on high. Cook butter, onion, and all seasonings on medium-high for 5 minutes. Add browned beef and continue cooking for 5 more minutes. Place taco burger mixture on buns, top with taco sauce, cheeses, lettuce and tomatoes.

I keep quart bags of ground beef in my freezer for a quick over night thaw when making this dish the following day.

Tater Tot
Breakfast Casserole

Serves 8

- ☐ 3 lb. bag tater tots
- ☐ 2 lb. breakfast sausage, cooked and drained
- ☐ 1 tsp. cayenne pepper
- ☐ 1 small yellow onion, diced
- ☐ 1 tsp. salt & pepper
- ☐ 1 c. green & red bell peppers, diced
- ☐ 1 c. whole milk
- ☐ 4 eggs
- ☐ 2 c. cheddar jack cheese
- ☐ 1 c. cheddar cheese

Brown sausage and remove from grease. Sauté onions and peppers in sausage renderings for 2 minutes and drain. Mix eggs with milk. Add sausage, onions, peppers, and seasonings to the eggs. Layer tater tots on bottom of lightly sprayed baking dish. Pour mixture over tater tots. Sprinkle with cheese. Cover and refrigerate overnight (minimum 8 hours). Cover and bake at 350 degrees 30 minutes. Uncover and bake another 20 minutes.

Our daughter, (Courtney) is amazing at making this dish. Yummy for both breakfast and dinner.

Baked Tuna Casserole

Serves 6

- ☐ 1 c. plain panko breadcrumbs
- ☐ 2 cans tuna, drained
- ☐ 1 can cream mushroom soup
- ☐ 1 can cream of chicken soup
- ☐ 8 oz. sour cream
- ☐ 1 lb. egg noodles, medium size
- ☐ 2 c. cheddar cheese
- ☐ 6 tbs. butter, reserve 2 tbs for panko
- ☐ 1 tsp. each pepper, onion powder, dill

Cook egg noodles per package instructions. Melt 4 tbs. butter and ½ c. panko in baking dish. Add remaining ingredients then pour into buttered baking dish. Cover with remaining ½ c. panko and 2 tbs. melted butter. Bake covered on 350 degrees for 30 minutes.

Have your favorite hot sauce ready!

Hamburger Gulash

Serves 6

- ☐ 2 lb. ground beef, sauteed
- ☐ 2 lbs. cooked pasta (elbow is best)
- ☐ 1 can whole kernel sweet corn, drained
- ☐ 2 tbs. ketchup
- ☐ 1 tsp. mustard
- ☐ 1 tsp. each garlic powder, onion powder, & dry mustard
- ☐ 1 tbs. olive oil
- ☐ 1 large jar of favorite pasta sauce
- ☐ 1 small can of tomato paste
- ☐ 4 c. shredded Cheddar cheese

Combine tomato paste, seasonings, pasta sauce, and olive oil into a saucepan. Heat on medium for 5 minutes. Add meat, pasta and sauce mixture. Pour into a 9x13 baking dish. Cover with cheese. Use cooking spray to coat the tinfoil cover and bake 350 degrees for 45 minutes uncover last 10 minutes.

One of my favorite cousins' Marsha and I would make this dish when we were young. My Aunt Linda taught us this recipe one summer when I visited their home in Tallahassee.

Quick Sweet Heat Chicken and Waffles

Serves 4

- ☐ 8 pieces of your favorite crispy chicken tenders
- ☐ 8 fluffy waffles, Belgium or freshly made
- ☐ 1 c. buttery syrup *(don't skimp on quality)
- ☐ ½ c. powdered sugar
- ☐ 1 tbs. Crystals hot sauce
- ☐ 1 tbs. fresh arugula for garnish
- ☐ 1 tsp. of red pepper flakes

Toast your Belgium waffles or make your waffles per the package instructions. Drizzle hot sauce on your crispy tenders before baking or air frying according to the labeled instructions. Once the chicken is ready, top the chicken on your hot waffles, drizzle with syrup. Garnish with powdered sugar, red pepper flakes and arugula.

Collard Greens

Serves 8

- [ ] 3 lbs. (3 or 4 bundles) fresh collards, washed and chopped
- [ ] 2 tsp. butter
- [ ] 1 tsp. garlic, minced
- [ ] 2 tbs. sugar
- [ ] 3 c. chicken stock
- [ ] 1 large smoked turkey leg
- [ ] 1 tsp. olive oil
- [ ] 1 tsp. each salt and pepper
- [ ] 1 tsp. white vinegar
- [ ] 1 tsp. lemon juice
- [ ] 1 ½ onions, minced

Pull meat from smoked turkey leg. Combine turkey meat, onions, garlic and olive oil in pot. Sauté for 5 minutes. Add remaining ingredients, cover and simmer for 1 hour. Last 10 minutes add vinegar.

Momma always served this dish with her amazing cornbread and pepper sauce. Put collard green juice in a bowl then add crumbled cornbread to make Southern Pot-liquor aka Southern Pot Likker.

Copper Pennies

Serves 6

- ☐ 6 large carrots, washed thoroughly
- ☐ 2 c. of water to boil
- ☐ ¼ stick of butter
- ☐ 1 c. dark brown sugar
- ☐ salt & pepper to taste

Slice carrots ¼ in. thick. Bring all ingredients to boil on high for 5 minutes, reduce to simmer for 15 mins until tender.

These carrots are quick fresh farm to table side dish year-round. Enjoy adding additional harvest flavors such as cinnamon, nutmeg, garlic, or tummeric.

Cornbread Bake

Serves 8

- ☐ 1 box of jiffy cornbread mix
- ☐ ½ c. vegetable oil
- ☐ 1 tbs. sugar
- ☐ 1 can sweet cream corn
- ☐ 1 tsp. salt and pepper
- ☐ 3 eggs, beaten
- ☐ 8 oz. sour cream

Preheat over 350. Mix all ingredients and pour into greased 9x13 pan. Bake 35 minutes.

I like to add fresh minced jalapenos for a touch of color and heat.

Cowboy BBQ Baked Beans

Serves 12

- ☐ 1 large onion, minced
- ☐ ¾ c. catsup
- ☐ ¼ c. yellow mustard
- ☐ ½ c. sweet BBQ sauce
- ☐ 1 tbs. lemon juice
- ☐ 2 large cans Bush's baked beans
- ☐ 1 tbs. Worchester sauce
- ☐ 4 slices of bacon cut into 1-inch pieces
- ☐ 1 lb. hamburger meat
- ☐ 1 tbs. flour
- ☐ 2 tbs. butter
- ☐ 1 c. brown sugar
- ☐ 1 tsp. each salt, pepper, and onion powder
- ☐ 1 tsp. of fresh minced garlic

Sautee the butter, bacon, garlic, and onions in pan. In a separate pan brown hamburger meat. Drain hamburger, reserving 1 tbs. of grease. Add flour to the grease stirring on low for a couple of minutes then add all remining ingredients. Toss the onions and bacon with the grease back into the mix. Transfer into a 9x13 baking dish. Cover and bake on 350 for 35 to 40 minutes.

Creamed Corn

Serves 6

- ☐ 5 c. frozen corn or fresh off the cob
- ☐ 2 tsp. butter
- ☐ 1 tbs. flour
- ☐ 2 c. half & half
- ☐ ½ tsp. garlic powder
- ☐ 1 tsp. each salt and pepper
- ☐ ½ tsp. paprika

Melt butter over medium heat, add flour stirring to make a roux. Whisk in half & half, garlic, and paprika stirring until smooth. Stir in corn, after 10 minutes turn heat to simmer. Stirring frequently, continue cooking on simmer for an additional 30 minutes.

The best option would be fresh corn cut off the cob, but if seasonal is not in, then frozen would be your best option. Mom shared this recipe and her creamed corn recipe taste exactly like my granny's did!

Field
Peas

Serves 6

- ☐ 1 lb. field peas
- ☐ 1 slice of thick ham, diced
- ☐ 2 cups of water (enough to cover peas 1 inch)
- ☐ 1 tsp. vegetable oil or bacon fat
- ☐ 1 tsp. each salt and pepper

Combine all ingredients in a saucepan. Bring to a boil, then simmer for 40 mins. Peas will not float when finished cooking.

These summer peas pair well with yellow rice as an additional side. If you wish to blanche them for freezing, bring peas to boil with enough water to cover. Once they come to a boil uncover, turn off heat and allow to cool to room temp. Place in quart freezer bags for up to 6 months.

Granny's Quick Green Beans

Serves 4

- ☐ 2 16oz. cans of green beans, drained
- ☐ 1 can cream of mushroom soup
- ☐ 2 tsp. butter
- ☐ 1 tsp. each salt and pepper
- ☐ 1 tsp. lemon juice
- ☐ 4 oz. French fried onions

Place beans in 9x9 casserole dish. Combine lemon juice, soup, and seasonings. Spread on top of green beans. Slice the butter thin on top before baking. Bake 350 for 30 minutes. Remove from heat and sprinkle with onions. Put back in oven for 5 additional minutes.

Hashbrown Casserole

Serves 8

- ☐ 2 lbs. shredded hash browns, thawed
- ☐ 1 stick butter, melted
- ☐ 1 can cream of chicken soup
- ☐ 1 can cream of mushroom soup
- ☐ 4 c. cheddar cheese or mixed, grated
- ☐ 1 tbs. Dijon mustard
- ☐ 1 tsp. pepper, garlic powder
- ☐ ½ tsp. salt
- ☐ 8 oz. sour cream
- ☐ ½ c. chopped onion
- ☐ Dash of hot sauce
- ☐ 2 sleeves Ritz crackers, crushed

Mix all ingredients in a large bowl, reserving the crackers. Pour potato mixture into greased 9x13 pan. Preheat oven to 400, bake 40-45 minutes.

Minced Jalapenos are always a nice way to create a bit of heat.

Home-Style Loaded Mashed Potatoes

Serves 6

- ☐ 8 medium Idaho potatoes, peeled and cubed small
- ☐ 1 stick butter, melted
- ☐ 4 oz. cream cheese, softened
- ☐ 1 c. half & half
- ☐ 2 c. cheddar cheese, grated
- ☐ 1 tsp. each salt, pepper, onion powder, garlic powder
- ☐ 8 oz. sour cream
- ☐ 8 slices of bacon, browned and chopped
- ☐ 2 green onions, sliced thin

Boil potatoes for 10-12 minutes and drain reserving 1 cup of liquid. In a large bowl mash potatoes and combine butter, cream cheese, half & half, seasonings, butter and sour cream. Pour into a greased baking dish. Cover with cheese and bacon. Cover with tinfoil, bake 350 for 30 minutes. Garnish with green onions.

Oven Roasted Okra

Serves 4

- ☐ 2 quarts fresh okra, medium not large
- ☐ 1 tsp. Worcestershire sauce
- ☐ ½ stick butter
- ☐ 2 tbs. vegetable oil or bacon fat
- ☐ 1 medium white onion, diced
- ☐ salt and pepper

Wash and slice okra ¼ inch slices. Heat butter and oil then add all ingredients. Cook on medium-high for 20 minutes, stirring often. Place okra in a greased baking dish then into preheated 350 degrees oven. Cover and bake for 30 minutes.

I use a cast iron skillet to cook on both stovetop and then in the oven.

This dish is my dear friend Melvin's favorite. He has been kicking cancer to the curb for many years. He is one of my heroes!!

Sauteed Cabbage

Serves 4

- ☐ 1 medium head of green cabbage, sliced thin
- ☐ 1 small onion, sliced thin
- ☐ 2 thick bacon slices, cut into inch pieces
- ☐ 3 tbs. butter, unsalted
- ☐ 2 tbs. granulated sugar
- ☐ 1 tsp. apple cider vinegar
- ☐ 1 tsp. each garlic powder and onion powder
- ☐ 2 c. chicken broth
- ☐ 1 tsp. each salt and black pepper

Wash and drain cabbage. Cook bacon and onions. Add cabbage into saucepan with bacon. Sauté for 10 minutes, add remaining ingredients. Cover and cook for 30 minutes or tender. Taste to see if you would prefer more salt or sugar.

Best have some pepper sauce near by to bring out the flavor of the cabbage.

Savory Sweet Potato Bake

Serves 8-12

- ☐ 4 sweet potatoes, diced
- ☐ 2 granny smith apples, diced
- ☐ 1 small sweet onion, minced
- ☐ 1 tsp. salt
- ☐ ½ tsp. black pepper
- ☐ 1 tbs. butter
- ☐ 1 tbs. olive oil
- ☐ Parsley to garnish

Sautee sweet onions in butter and olive oil. Bring potatoes to boil then turn them off. Let potatoes sit for 5 minutes. Combine all ingredients into a lightly greased 10x13 pan. Cover and bake on 350 for 30 minutes.

Mom shared this one. It will surprise you. I like adding 1 tbs. of brown sugar to my sweet potatoes.

Scalloped Potatoes

Serves 6

- ☐ 6 potatoes, large and sliced
- ☐ 1 small, sweet onion, sliced
- ☐ 1 c. evaporated milk
- ☐ 1 tsp. salt
- ☐ ½ tsp. black pepper
- ☐ 1 tsp. paprika for topping
- ☐ 4 tbs. butter, sliced

Sautee sweet onions in butter and olive oil. Bring potatoes to boil then turn them off. Let potatoes sit for 5 minutes. Combine all ingredients into a lightly greased 10x13 pan. Cover and bake on 350 for 30 minutes. Uncover and bake an additional 15 minutes.

I like adding sour cream and chives topping my scalloped potatoes. Mom made these and I could eat her scalloped potatoes until I would burst.

Sweet Potato Souffle

Serves 4

- ☐ 1 large can sweet potatoes, mashed
- ☐ 1 c. sugar
- ☐ 1 stick of butter
- ☐ 2 eggs
- ☐ 1 tsp. vanilla extract
- ☐ ½ tsp. salt

Toppings:

- ☐ 1 c. packed light brown sugar
- ☐ 1/3 c. all-purpose flour
- ☐ 1 c. pecans, chopped
- ☐ 1 stick of butter

Combine potatoes, sugar, 1 stick of butter, vanilla, salt and eggs in a bowl mix well. Pour into a 9x13 greased baking dish. Combine topping ingredients and sprinkle over potato mixture. Bake in preheated 350 oven for 30 minutes.

My favorite side at Thanksgiving. My Granny Tillman shared this recipe. That sweet lady had the God given talent to make anything from her kitchen and it would never disappoint!

Turnip Greens

Serves 4

- [ ] 2 bunches of young turnip greens with roots
- [ ] ½ c. chicken broth
- [ ] 1 c. water
- [ ] 1 tbs. bacon fat
- [ ] 1 tbs. olive oil
- [ ] 1 tsp. each salt & pepper
- [ ] 1 tbs. sugar
- [ ] 1 tsp. apple cider vinegar

Separate the stems from the leaves and roots. Discard stems. Wash leaves (5) five times ensuring no dirt or sand is on the leaves. Wash, peel and thinly slice the roots. Add all ingredients to the stock pot. Bring to a boil for 10 minutes, then reduce heat for 2 hours or until tender.

Pepper sauce is perfect sprinkled on top.

Mushroom Rice

Serves 4-6

- ☐ 3 ½ c. water
- ☐ 2 c. rice, white
- ☐ 2 beef bouillon cubes
- ☐ 1 c. mushrooms, diced
- ☐ 1 small onion, diced
- ☐ 1 stick butter
- ☐ ½ tsp. onion powder. garlic salt, pepper
- ☐ ½ tsp. reduced sodium or regular soy sauce

Heat rice in skillet until lightly brown, then add rice with remaining ingredients to rice cooker or bake in oven 350 degrees 30 minutes. Using rice cooker set to "white rice". If baking in oven, use boiling water then add all ingredients.

Use par-boiled rice for best results.

Squash Casserole

Serves 4

- ☐ 2 c. yellow squash, thinly sliced
- ☐ 2 c. Ritz Crackers, crushed fine
- ☐ 1 can cream of mushroom soup
- ☐ 1 c. evaporated milk
- ☐ 1 ½ c. cheddar cheese, shredded
- ☐ 1 c. small white onion, diced
- ☐ 1 stick of butter
- ☐ 2 eggs, slightly beaten
- ☐ 1 tsp. each salt, pepper and sugar

Combine 1 cup of Ritz cracker crumbs, milk, cheese and onion. In a separate bowl mix egg, butter, sugar, cream of mushroom, salt and pepper. Combine both mixtures and toss in squash. Pour in a 8x8 buttered casserole dish and top with remaining Ritz crackers. Cover and bake at 350 degrees for 40 minutes.

Tomato and Okra Gravy

Serves 4

- ☐ 1 lb. okra, sliced thin
- ☐ 2 large tomatoes, diced
- ☐ 1 small onion, sliced thin
- ☐ 2 slices of thick bacon, cut into inch pieces
- ☐ 3 tbs. butter, unsalted
- ☐ 2 tbs. granulated sugar
- ☐ 1 tsp. apple cider vinegar
- ☐ 1 tsp. each garlic powder and onion powder
- ☐ 2 c. vegetable broth
- ☐ 1 tsp. each salt and black pepper

Wash and slice okra then set aside. Sautee bacon and onions until onions are translucent. Add okra to bacon mixture and cook an additional 10 minutes. Add tomatoes into saucepan with other ingredients. Cover and cook for 30 minutes or tender. Taste to see if you would prefer more salt or sugar.

Best served with some pepper sauce and biscuits.

Butter Beans

Serves 4

- ☐ 1 lb. fresh butter beans
- ☐ 2 thick slices of bacon, cut into inch pieces
- ☐ 3 tbs. butter, unsalted
- ☐ 4 tbs. granulated sugar
- ☐ 1 tsp. each garlic powder and onion powder
- ☐ water to cover
- ☐ 1 tsp. each salt and black pepper

Wash and drain butter beans. Add into saucepan. Next cover the beans with water (an inch over the beans). Add remaining ingredients to the beans. Bring to a boil then turn to a simmer for 45 minutes or tender. Taste to see if you would prefer more salt or sugar.

Butter beans pair well with chicken, ham, or beef. Our daughter, Courtney loves these with a side of fluffy steamed rice.

Desserts

Blackberry Dumplings

Cook 20 mins

- [ ] 2 quarts of washed blackberries
- [ ] 4 cups of water to boil
- [ ] 2 .5 cups of sugar

Dumplings:

- [ ] 2.5 cups self-rising flour
- [ ] 1 cup of lard or Crisco
- [ ] 1 cup buttermilk
- [ ] 2 tbls sugar
- [ ] 1 tsp vanilla extract

Bring water, berries and 2 cups of sugar to boil. Quickly turn down temp to low boil for 10 mins. Begin dumplings in a large bowl by adding flour and lard. Mix with hands until the dough becomes flaky then add buttermilk, vanilla, and sugar mix with hands or fork ONLY. It will be very sticky and wet add more buttermilk if it is too dry and not tacky sticky. Remove all berries from the boiling liquid and set aside. Add a dollop (teaspoon) of the dumpling mixture to the boiling berries and DO NOT STIR. Return berries, cover and simmer for 10 mins (gently move liquid around dumplings) with a fork.

I have such wonderful memories of when my Granny Slay made this delicious summer-time dessert. It is a cost effective dessert. Sometimes Granny would add ice cream on top. Such a special treat to share with all my cousins on the weekends.

Blueberry Cobbler

Serves 8

- [ ] 2 c. canned or fresh blueberry pie filling
- [ ] 1 c. sugar
- [ ] 1 c. flour
- [ ] 1 c. whole milk (not evaporated)
- [ ] 1 stick of butter (melted in the pan)
- [ ] 1 tsp. vanilla extract

Mix sugar and flour. Add milk and vanilla extract to the dry mix of flour and sugar. Pour batter into 9x13 pan over the melted butter. Spoon drop the pie filling equally portioned on top of the batter.

Bake in a pre-heated 350-degree oven for 45 minutes. If the edges become dark and the middle still jiggles when you shake, cover the edges with foil to protect from burning. Allow to cool for 5 minutes and then serve with ice cream. Allow to chill in a 10x13 baking dish.

Pie filling can be used of your choice such as cherry or apple.

Fresh Blueberry Pie Filling

Serves 8

- ☐ 3 c. blueberries
- ☐ 1 c. sugar
- ☐ 2 ½ tbs. cornstarch
- ☐ ¼ tsp. salt
- ☐ ½ c. water
- ☐ 1 tbs. butter
- ☐ 1 tbs. lemon juice (fresh squeezed)
- ☐ ½ stick butter, melted

Blend sugar, salt, and cornstarch in a saucepan. Add water stirring constantly until clear. Add 1 c. berries stirring until mixture is blue color. Add lemon and butter. Cook the remaining berries for 5 minutes. Allow to chill in a 10x13 baking dish.

Enjoy topped on a pie, pound cake, or ice cream dessert.

Mini Pumpkin Bread

Serves 6

- [ ] 2 c. pumpkin puree
- [ ] 1 c. Crisco oil
- [ ] 3 c. sugar
- [ ] 4 eggs, large
- [ ] 3 ½ c. *SR flour
- [ ] 2 tsp. pumpkin pie spice
- [ ] 1 tsp. ground cinnamon
- [ ] 1 tsp. honey

Mix oil and sugar, slowly add flour then eggs. Blend pumpkin, honey and spices together in separate bowl. Bake in small muffin loaves 350 degrees for 35 minutes or until toothpick comes clean from the center.

Mom taught me to sprinkle turbinado aka raw cane sugar crystals on top of the warm dessert breads.

Zucchini Bread

Mini Loaves

- ☐ 2 c. Zucchini, grated
- ☐ 1 c. Crisco oil
- ☐ 2 c. sugar
- ☐ 3 eggs, large, beaten
- ☐ 3 c. *SR flour
- ☐ 1 tsp. salt
- ☐ 1 tsp. ground cinnamon
- ☐ 3 tsp. vanilla

Mix all together except zucchini. Fold in zucchini once all is blended smooth. Bake in small muffin loaves 350 degrees for 45 minutes or until toothpick comes clean from the center.

If you prefer you could add 1 c. chopped nuts.

Breakfast Biscuits

Serves 8-10

- ☐ 3 c. sifted *AP All Purpose flour
- ☐ 3 tbs. sugar
- ☐ 2 tbs. *BP baking powder
- ☐ ½ tsp. salt
- ☐ ½ c. cold unsalted butter, grated
- ☐ ¾ c. whole milk, cold

Mix wet to dry. Kneed and flatten on floured surface no more than 3 times. Cut with lid rings of pint size jars. Oil iron skillet, place biscuit one at a time close together, but not touching. Preheat 450 degrees, bake 15 minutes or until golden brown.

Try adding a pat of butter which will melt on a warm biscuit. My grandmothers would drizzle honey on their biscuits. I love adding thick ham slices with local honey.

Easy No-Bake Cherry Pie

Serves 8

- ☐ 1 can cherry Pie filling
- ☐ 1 container of cool whip
- ☐ 8 oz. cream cheese, room temperature
- ☐ 1 can condensed milk
- ☐ 1 tsp. vanilla extract
- ☐ 1 graham cracker pie crust

Pour Cherry filling into pie crust. Mix remaining ingredients for 2 minutes then add on top of the cherry pie filling. Freeze for 4 hours and before serving.

Pie filling can be used of your choice such as blueberry or apple.

Never Fail Divinity

Serves 8

- ☐ ½ c. water
- ☐ 2 c. sugar
- ☐ Pinch of salt
- ☐ 1 (7oz) jar marshmallow cream
- ☐ ¼ c. chopped nuts

Combine water, sugar, and salt. Bring to a rolling boil and boil for 2 minutes ONLY. Place cream in a bowl and pour hot syrup over it. Stir until candy loses gloss then add nuts. Drop from spoon onto waxed paper.

Peanut Butter & Toffee Pie

Serves 8

- ☐ 6 oz. cream cheese, softened
- ☐ 1 container of thawed cool whip
- ☐ 1 small package of crushed Heath toffee candy
- ☐ ¾ c. sifted powdered sugar
- ☐ ½ c. peanut butter
- ☐ 2 tbs. milk
- ☐ 1 graham cracker crust

Beat together cream cheese, sugar, milk and peanut butter until smooth and creamy, then fold in cool whip. Cover graham cracker crust with ½ crushed Heath candy. Add peanut butter mixture into pie shell. Sprinkle remaining Heath candy on top. Chill for 6-8 hours.

Our family friend, (Jeff Moore) loves this dessert. He is diabetic but would cheat with this dessert! Sometimes I sprinkle in some butterscotch morsels to the pie filling.

Pecan Pie

Serves 8

- ☐ 3 eggs
- ☐ 1 c. brown sugar
- ☐ 1.5 c. pecans, chopped
- ☐ 1 c. Karo syrup
- ☐ 1 tsp. vanilla
- ☐ ½ tsp. Salt
- ☐ 2 tbs. butter
- ☐ 1 pie crust, unbaked

Combine syrup, eggs, sugar, salt, vanilla, and butter in a bowl. Stir in pecans. Pour into an unbaked pie shell. Bake in preheated 350 degrees for 60 minutes. Should crust edges begin to darken past your liking, cover with strips of foil to protect from burning.

Snicker Doodles

Makes 6 dozen

- ☐ 1 c. water
- ☐ 1 ½ c. sugar
- ☐ 2 eggs, room temperature
- ☐ 2 ¾ c. *AP flour
- ☐ 1 tsp. soda
- ☐ ¼ tsp. salt
- ☐ 2 tsp. cinnamon
- ☐ 2 tsp. sugar

Mix the first 3 ingredients. Add the next 4 ingredients ONLY, reserve the last 2 ingredients. Shape dough into 1-inch balls and roll into mixture of 2T. sugar and 2 T. cinnamon. Put in the refrigerator and chill for 30 minutes before baking. Preheat oven to 400 degrees. Bake for 8-10 minutes.

*My bestie Deborah makes these cookies with a different recipe. I don't know how she makes her cookies taste like fluffy pillows.

Granny's Sour Cream Pound Cake

Serves 8

- ☐ 6 large eggs, room temp
- ☐ 2 ½ sticks butter, room temp
- ☐ 3 c. sugar
- ☐ 3 c. all-purpose flour, sifted
- ☐ ½ tsp. baking soda
- ☐ 1 tsp. salt
- ☐ 1 c. sour cream, room temp
- ☐ 2 tsp. almond extract
- ☐ 1 tsp. vanilla extract, pure

Cream butter in mixer alternate adding in sugar and 1 egg at a time to emulsify. Beat for about 4 minutes on medium speed. Add extracts of almond and vanilla continuing mixing (switch to low) for another 2 minutes. Add flour, salt and baking soda. Lastly, fold in room temp sour cream. Bake in floured bundt pan 325 degrees for 80-90 minutes

My Great Aunt Alma never preheated her oven and only baked on a Full Moon!

NUGGET-Resting the pan on a damp towel to help loosen the cake off the bottom of pan.

OPTONAL- Add a lemon glaze (1 cup confection sugar and 1 tsp lemon juice)

Strawberry Butter

Serves 6

- ☐ 1 c. butter
- ☐ ½ c. honey
- ☐ ½ c. fresh strawberries, pulsed in blender

Cream butter in mixer until fluffy. Blend in small amounts of honey at a time, then fold in strawberries. Perfect on warm corn muffins for that balance of sweet and salty.

Addy's Fresh Fruit Pizza

Serves 8

- ☐ 1 large roll of sugar cookie dough
- ☐ 8 oz. cream cheese, softened
- ☐ 1 pint fresh strawberries, rinsed, dried and sliced
- ☐ 1 pint fresh blueberries, rinsed and dried
- ☐ 2 kiwis, peeled and sliced thin
- ☐ 2 tangerines, pulled apart
- ☐ 1 stick unsalted butter, softened
- ☐ 2 tbs. whole milk
- ☐ 1 tsp. vanilla extract

Slice sugar cookie dough and evenly press in 12-inch pizza pan. Bake 325 for 15-20 minutes. Allow to cool completely. Mix cream cheese, vanilla, and butter. Slowly incorporate confectioner sugar with hand mixer or electric mixing bowl. Spread the cream cheese mixture on the cooled cookie. Next arrange the fresh fruit rotating in circular design alternating between your fruit of choice.

Use any fruit you love to décor your pizza. Our granddaughter Addyson fascinates us with her creativity decorating her pizzas!!

Angel Food and Fruit Trifle

Serves 8

- ☐ 1 angel food cake, fresh baked
- ☐ 6 c. fresh fruit, blueberries, raspberry, and strawberries
- ☐ 2 c. cool whip or heavy whipping cream
- ☐ 2 tsp. vanilla extract
- ☐ 1 c. powder sugar
- ☐ 2 vanilla pudding packages

Prepare pudding per instructions. Next beat powdered sugar, half and half and vanilla on high-speed until stiff peaks.

Cut the cake into small 1-inch pieces. Next clean and wash fruit. Allow fruit to dry. Begin layering the clear serving bowl. Start layering with cake on the bottom, next pudding, fruit, cream. Continue repeating.

Mint leaves are an adorable decor with cool whip in the center.
Thankful to my dear Christian mentor Chef Bob who taught me this recipe and many more. #GodBless

Rhubarb Pie

Serves 8

- ☐ 3 eggs, yolks only, beaten
- ☐ 3 c. rhubarb, diced
- ☐ 1.5 c. sugar
- ☐ 3 tbs. flour
- ☐ ½ tsp. nutmeg
- ☐ 1 tbs. butter
- ☐ 1 tsp. vanilla
- ☐ ¼ tsp. Salt

Combine eggs and sugar then add flour, butter, vanilla, salt, and nutmeg. Mix well then incorporate rhubarb. Pour all ingredients into an unbaked pie shell. Bake 350 degrees for 40 minutes.

Fresh Fruit
Salad

Serves 8

- ☐ 1 pint blueberries
- ☐ 1 pint sliced strawberries
- ☐ 1 c. chopped pineapple
- ☐ 1 c. each red and green grapes (seedless)
- ☐ 1 pint each raspberries and blackberries
- ☐ 3 trimmed and sliced kiwis
- ☐ ½ trimmed and diced watermelon or honey dew
- ☐ 2 c. pitted cherries
- ☐ 1 c. raw cane sugar (turbinado)

Layer pineapple on the bottom of bowl. Next layer all your fruit or mix it all together. Sprinkle sugar on top.

Mom taught me to sprinkle turbinado, aka raw cane sugar crystals on top of the fruit. This is very pretty and so delightful.

Charlie's Strawberry Shake

Serves 4

- ☐ 6 c. vanilla bean ice cream
- ☐ 2 c. fresh strawberries
- ☐ 1 c. frozen sliced strawberries, pureed
- ☐ 1 c. milk
- ☐ 1 can whipped cream
- ☐ 2 tbs. rainbow sprinkles

Remove strawberry stems, wash and set aside. Add pureed strawberries into the bottom of each glass (divided equally). In a blender, combine milk, ice cream, and fresh strawberries (reserving 1 each for toppings). Pour ice cream shake mixture in glass. Top with whipped cream, sprinkles and a strawberry for the finishing touch.

Add a small amount of any fresh fruit such as blueberries if you desire.

This is our granddaughter's (Charlie) favorite!! She could eat strawberries dusk to dawn everyday if allowed.

www.ingramcontent.com/pod-product-compliance
Lightning Source LLC
Chambersburg PA
CBHW051627140626
46547CB00033B/2735